COOKING OUT OF
THIS WORLD

Also by Anne McCaffrey
from The Wildside Press:

Rescue Run

COOKING OUT OF THIS WORLD

Edited by
Anne McCaffrey

The Wildside Press
Newark, NJ ❧ 1992

This edition published by:

The Wildside Press
37 Fillmore Street
Newark, NJ 07105

For a complete list of currently available books from Wildside, including other titles by Anne McCaffrey, send a self-addressed, stamped envelope to the above address.

Cover art by Pat Morrissey.

ISBN: 1-880448-13-0

10 9 8 7 6 5 4 3 2

Printed in the U.S.A.

Dedicated respectfully to
Eathaline Robinson,
a superb cook

CONTENTS

INVITATION TO THE DINNER
by Tom Disch

All right, everybody, let's sit down
To dinner. Mike, you may pass
The potatoes. Hilary, is there any
Gloucestershire sauce? Thank you. John,
That's your place, and this is mine.
I'm so hungry and everything looks so good!
Art has an important part in all our lives,
But it is never as important as dinner.
That is why I have made this poem a dinner
And invited you to it.

BRIAN ALDISS

Margaret Aldiss writes:

Brian's cooking is nowhere near the same category as his writing, but he's great at providing encouragement and appreciation, and is expert at things like poppadums (what is like a poppadum. . . ?).

When we spent six months traveling all over Yugoslavia, in the happy days before we got married, Brian was writing a travel book — *Cities and Stones*, published by Faber & Faber — and I was collecting recipes. My cookbook did not materialize, possibly because we were not very inspired by the food, but one of the recipes we do like is —

Alasi Corba, Fishermen's Soup
(*alasi* being Serbian river fishermen)

3 lbs. mixed small fish, or fish trimmings

$\frac{3}{4}$ lb. finely chopped onions

handful parsley, handful chopped celery

$\frac{1}{2}$ lb. chopped tomatoes, or small tin

1 chopped green pepper

2 lbs. large fish

2 egg yolks

2 tbsp. wine vinegar

6 slices crisp toast

bay leaf and seasoning

Clean and trim small fish, lay in large pan and cover with chopped onions, tomatoes, pepper, herbs, and seasoning. Fill the pan with cold water, bring to boil and simmer for about 45 minutes. Strain the stock and return to the pan. Add the large fish in pieces and simmer again for about 20 minutes. Beat the egg yolks with the vinegar in a tureen and add the soup. Ladle into soup plates over a piece of hot crisp toast.

Our favorite recipe at the moment follows — it's delicious and looks good, too; Brian can be found eating up the leftover rice and sauce at any time of day or night!

Risotto al Pollo, Chicken Risotto

1 boiling chicken, about 5 lbs.	4 oz. grated Parmesan cheese
2 onions	2 level tbsp. flour
1 lb. Italian rice	salt, pepper, bay leaves, nutmeg
$\frac{1}{2}$ pint milk	
4 oz. butter	$\frac{1}{4}$ pint single cream

Simmer the chicken in a deep pan with enough water to cover, 1 onion, 3 bay leaves, salt, and 4 peppercorns, until very tender. Then melt 2 oz. butter in a large sauté pan and fry the other onion, chopped, until transparent. Add the rice and stir for 2 minutes over gentle heat. Add enough chicken stock to cover and simmer until it is absorbed. Continue adding stock until the rice is tender — *al dente* — then spread the rice over a large ovenware dish or ashet. Take the chicken off the bone and lay in neat pieces all over the rice.

Then make the sauce: Melt the remaining 2 oz. butter in a

saucepan, and add the flour; blend well and cook for 2 minutes. Add the milk gradually, and then enough chicken stock to make a smooth sauce, not too thick. Season with salt, pepper, and a good pinch of nutmeg. Add the Parmesan cheese and the cream, and stir over a very low heat until the sauce is smooth. Pour over the chicken and rice to cover it, and heat through in a moderate oven until lightly browned on top. This can be made in advance and heated up before serving.

The dish I most want to have the recipe for is a dessert we eat when we dine in style with Brian's publisher, Charles Monteith, at All Souls' College, surrounded by the college silver and other eminent writers published by Fabers like Harry Harrison and Jim Blish! The nearest I can get to it is as follows, but the chef at All Souls' manages to freeze it and produce it standing proudly in a platter:

Atholl Brose

(Really a good Scots drink, but here a kind of mousse.)

Beat $1\frac{1}{2}$ cups of double cream to a froth, and stir in a cup of lightly toasted oatmeal. Add half a cup of clear heather honey and 2 wineglasses of Scotch whiskey. Mix well, and serve in shallow glasses.

KAREN ANDERSON

Osaka "Baked" Beans

1 lb. Kuromame (black
Japanese beans)

$\frac{1}{2}$ lb. bacon, thick-sliced

$\frac{1}{2}$ cup sugar

$\frac{1}{2}$ cup shoyu
(Japanese-style soy
sauce)

Soak Kuromame overnight and simmer with salt to taste until tender. Fry bacon, preferably in a cast-iron (large) skillet, pouring off and reserving fat as it accumulates. When the bacon is done, drain and add the beans with sugar, shoyu, and about half of reserved bacon fat. Cook together until liquid is reduced. Correct seasoning to taste. Serves 6.

Elves', Gnomes', Leprechauns', and Little Men's Chowder

In four quarts cold water bring to a boil:

$\frac{1}{4}$ cup Accent

4 oz. Hana Katsuo (shaved dried bonito)

4 oz. Ise-Hijiki or a substitute, such as 2 oz. sheet Nori (20 sheets)

(Note: Ise-Hijiki and Nori are two kinds of seaweed)

$\frac{3}{4}$ cup salt

$1\frac{1}{2}$ tsp. Shichimi Togarishi — Japanese chili powder

(Note: Shichimi Togarishi is a spice mixture, about 50 percent red pepper)

Simmer gently for ten minutes and strain. Discard solids.

In 4 oz. olive oil fry 4 lbs. chopped onion.

To the dashi-broth above add:

the fried onions

10 lbs. potatoes, cubed

10 lbs. carrots, sliced

On top place:

1 bunch leeks

$\frac{1}{4}$ bunch parsley

water q.s. (just enough to float everything so it won't stick)

Cook until tender. Discard leeks and parsley.

At this point it may be advisable to divide the ingredients and use a second kettle.

To the above stew add:

5 lbs. pear tomatoes, canned, cut up

2 tbsp. basil

3 or 4 garlic cloves, sliced

juice of 12 lbs. minced canned clams (25 cans); set clams aside (refrigerate)

Simmer gently for an hour.

This may be left overnight. When ready to use, bring to a boil and add the clams.

Yield: 6-7 gallons.

Szekely Yaki

1 pkg. egg noodles

2 lbs. stew beef

1 lb. stew lamb

3 lge. cloves of garlic

1 bunch of leeks, cut up

$\frac{1}{2}$ cup cheap red wine

$\frac{1}{2}$ pint sour cream

$\frac{1}{2}$ lb. snow peas, cut up

$\frac{1}{4}$ cup shoyu (soy sauce)

2 small heads of bok-choy, cut up (Swiss chard, cut in $\frac{1}{2}$ inch slices, may be used)

1 lb. of bean sprouts (or thin sliced celery)

1 block of tofu (bean curd,) cut up

$\frac{1}{4}$ lb. fresh mushrooms

Cut the meat in 2-inch pieces and brown in a hot skillet. Add the garlic, cut in small pieces, and pressure-cook with the wine for 20 minutes or until tender. Return to the frying pan and add shoyu, tofu, leeks, bok-choy, and bean sprouts. Cover and cook over a high flame, stirring occasionally, for about ten minutes. Add mushrooms and cook for 30 seconds longer. Serve over boiled noodles and top with sour cream. Serves 6.

Chowder (serves 3-4)

1 lb. cod, haddock, or whatever

1 small onion, chopped

2 tbsp. butter

3 thinly sliced potatoes

1 cup water

2 cups milk

1 8-oz. can corn — or fresh equivalent is better yet

$1\frac{1}{2}$ tsp. salt

$\frac{1}{4}$ tsp. fresh-ground pepper

turmeric, oregano, and dill to taste

Sauté onion in butter in kettle till soft. Add potatoes, fish, and water. Cover and simmer half an hour, adding the seasonings at this time. Then stir in everything else and heat to barely boiling.

Eggs

Turmeric does wonders for scrambled eggs; I also like to throw in some chopped scallion, chives, or whatever. Tabasco sauce is fine on poached eggs.

Cheese Garbanzos

I cook more by tongue and eyeball than by measure, so can't be too exact here. However:

In frying pan or fireproof dish, cook two or three slices of bacon, cut-up. Pour off most fat. Sauté one large onion, chopped. Add one large can of garbanzos, or equivalent in cooked fresh ones; one small can tomato paste, or two or three tomatoes blanched and cooked down to paste; a bit of water if needed to thin it all out; fairly generous sprinklings of parsley and rosemary, depending on how strong a flavor is desired; and salt to taste. Simmer till sauce begins to thicken. Cover with thick slices of cheese, sufficient to pretty well cover the top of the pan, and sprinkle generously with paprika. Bake a few minutes at ca. 400° F. till cheese melts. Should serve two to four, depending on appetites.

The Society for Creative Anachronism has generated a lot of interest in Medieval and Renaissance cookery — you should have seen a wedding reception we gave on our lawn, everybody in period dress, banners flying, and such dishes as urchins and a cockatrice prepared by Karen! — but as far as I know, thus far everything is taken out of existing, though old, books. Thought I'd pass on a recipe for mead, which is delicious, worked out by one member.

Mead

5 lbs. honey, 25 pints (a little more than 8 gallons) water, one orange or lemon, brewer's yeast (1 pkg.). Dissolve honey in water in a clean crock; add cut-up fruit; ginger is also good to put in for a flavor variation. Float the yeast on a couple pieces of toast so it won't drown before starting fermentation. Cover (with ventilation, e.g., a piece of cheesecloth) and leave at room temperature until fermentation stops, usually one to two weeks. Bottle. Unlike the sticky-sweet stuff usually sold, this comes out light, dry, and delicious.

Bachelor Pea Soup

Make canned pea soup with milk instead of water. Add a small can of corn and a small can of Vienna sausage (including the juice), chopped up. Grind in pepper to taste. Simmer. A hearty, quickly prepared meal for one or two.

Sjömansböf (Sailor Hash)

2 cups leftover roast beef, cubed
2 cups cold boiled potatoes, cubed
5 slices bacon
One *large* onion, cubed
Seasonings

Fry bacon crisp, drain on paper towel, dice. In the fat, gently fry onion till it is brown. Mix ingredients, season with salt, plenty of pepper, Worcestershire or soya sauce, or other condiments to taste. Add a little extra bacon grease and cook lightly together.

Spaghetti Meat Sauce

Sauté chopped onion, add ground meat, garlic, salt, pepper; cook lightly. Add tomato paste but use red wine instead of water for liquid and throw in fresh rosemary. Simmer.

Concerning Veal and Venison Sevagram

Yearling deer is hard to come by, especially if one believes that game laws are good and should be obeyed. But some areas do allow a limited occasional take, also in that age bracket, for the sake of thinning populations which would otherwise over-graze themselves into starvation.

Or you might luck out, as we did.

We had been to a New Year's Eve party, the kind from which nobody drives home till next day after sleeping awhile on the floor. I got back utterly wretched. Karen was all right, and wanted to accept an invitation we had to an afternoon gathering. So she left me with my hangover and drove off across the forested hills which separate our home from the cities along San Francisco Bay. Along about eight in the evening I was stretched out on the living room couch, beginning to come halfway back to health, when she returned. "Look what I found!" she exclaimed gleefully, and dropped this dead yearling deer on the rug. It had obviously been hit, and instantly killed, by a car not very long before.

I turned green, barely managed to string it up from the garage rafters, and left the rest to her. She'd never dressed anything larger than a chicken before, but managed quite well.

It *was* mildly illegal. You are supposed to report such finds to the game wardens, who then do something or other with them. But neither of us could see how we would damage the ecology by eating this beast ourselves. Our main problem was that we lacked a freezer at the time, and here was more meat than we could get around to before it spoiled.

So Karen took the haunches to Tony Boucher's house and offered them to him on condition that he invite us to the dinner. He, a lifetime gourmet, spent the next couple of days studying his vast collection of cookbooks. Not only could he find no recipe for this kind of veal, he could find no two alike for regular venison. So he worked up the following himself. It was superb.

If ever you do get a chance at some yearling deer, raise a glass of your best wine to the memory of Tony Boucher.

Anthony Boucher's
Venison Sevagram

(Jan. 7, 1963 — compiled from many sources, especially Morrison Wood and James Beard.)

2 legs of young deer, each 6 lbs. 2 oz.

Marinate approximately 40 hours, turning and basting every 4-6 hours.

Marinade:

1 fifth dry red wine (I used Concannon Livermore red)

$\frac{1}{2}$ cup olive oil

2 oz. cognac

1 medium onion

6 shallots

3 cloves garlic

3 slender carrots

2 bay leaves

2 blades mace

1 tbsp. parsley

1 tsp. dry hot mustard

1 tsp. powdered orange peel

6 juniper berries, crushed

$\frac{1}{2}$ tsp. each:

   thyme

   marjoram

   tarragon

   basil

   rosemary

   coriander

   peppercorns

   turmeric

Chop vegetables coarsely. Use whole, not ground, herbs (except turmeric and mustard), rubbed before adding.

Remove venison from marinade. Dry. Insert slivers of garlic (2 cloves). Salt and flour lightly on both sides. Top with 6 large pieces of salt pork. Preheat oven to 450° F. Brown for 15 min., turn and brown another 15 min. Reduce heat to 325° F. Meanwhile strain and heat marinade, which will (or at least did) need skimming and re-straining as it heats. Baste meat frequently (about every 20 min.) with warm marinade. On this occasion the marinade ran out and I replenished it with:

1 cup red wine (Martini Barbera)

1 can condensed beef bouillon

Cook for a total (including original browning) of 22 min. per lb. for medium/medium rare. At end of cooking time, remove meat and leave in warm unlit oven while making gravy.

Gravy:

To remaining marinade and juices in pan, add:

1 10-oz. jar currant jelly

Let melt completely, stirring occasionally, and add:

2 tbsp. cornstarch

Simmer 5-10 min. and serve.

POUL ANDERSON

All My Own Invention

2 oz. dark rum, 2 oz. dry vermouth, 1 oz. fresh lemon juice, stirred over ice. Sneaky.

BETTY BALLANTINE

Chicken Rufus

4 breasts of chicken, boned and cut up (or if you're feeling lazy, don't bone — just halve and halve again. But warn your guests to watch out for slivers) (and don't on any account give any to the dog) (use a heavy skillet). 1 big onion, cut up and sautéed with two crushed cloves garlic. Use two strips of bacon, or a couple tablespoons soy oil. Add your chicken pieces when the onion is transparent. Medium heat. Cook it around a bit, and then add:

1 tsp. paprika	4 sliced carrots
1 heaping tsp. oregano (or sweet basil if you like a more subtle flavor)	6 grapes
	$\frac{1}{2}$ cup sesame seeds

Mix around.

Now add 2 heaping tsps. protein powder, or soy flour, or even regular flour. Mix. This is to help the gravy.

Add $\frac{3}{4}$ cup red wine (*dry*). Mix, cover, and simmer over low heat for $\frac{1}{2}$ hour. When you are ready to serve (it can be right away, or several hours later) reheat gently, having added $\frac{1}{2}$ pt. yogurt. Or sour cream if you don't mind calories. And salt — don't forget the salt to taste, as they say.

Serve with baked potato, or with rice-lentil-peas mix, or anything that absorbs the gravy. Crunchy hot wholewheat bread. And a young red wine, because this is a rich dish that needs something gripping to cut it. Feeds about 8 sometimes.

Chicken Bearsville

In contrast to Chicken Rufus, a light and lovesome dish and a leadpipe cinch to make:

same heavy skillet
same 4 breasts of chicken, cut as before
same big onion and garlic sautéed in oil (*not* bacon)

Now your chicken is a nice, light brown. Add orange juice — enough to just barely cover. This can be fresh juice or juice made from frozen concentrate, but in the latter case only dilute by half. Leave the thing uncovered and simmering quietly until juice is reduced to a gravy — about twenty minutes to a half hour. This will give you a delicate sweet-and-sour chicken. Good with crunchy Chinese vegetables and plain rice, or a rice/peas mix.

My Rice

Heavy skillet. Cook 1 small cut-up onion in 2 tbsp. oil until transparent. Add one cup dry, uncooked rice (Uncle Ben's Converted is best). Coat the rice with oil. Add: 6 whole cloves, half a stick cinnamon, four cracked pods cardamom. Mix. Turn heat *way* down (if you're using electric, insert an asbestos pad between burner and skillet). Add enough *hot* water or stock to cover rice thoroughly. It will fuss up in a great cloud of steam. Don't be alarmed. Cover skillet securely and leave for fifteen minutes. Mix again, and check, i.e., bite on a couple of grains of the rice.

If it seems too *al dente*, add another half cup of liquid; cover and allow to absorb. Five minutes before serving, add package of frozen peas which have been thawed while all this is going on. Mix in thoroughly.

ALFRED BESTER

Here is a short essay on Fire Island cooking, incorporating two of my favorite recipes. I only wish there was space enough to include more of my favorites: The Art of the Clam Chowder, Together with a Guide to Shucking Clams; The Mystery of Bay Scallops and How to Outwit Them; Large Lobsters, Whither?; Of Time and Bluefish; etc. etc. etc.

One last pathetic note: Great South Bay, which bounds the north side of Fire Island and where I spent so many happy summers fishing, clamming, oystering, and lobstering, is now so completely polluted by mainland sewage that it's no longer safe to eat anything that it contains. Alas! Alas! Alas! As a friend of my undergraduate years once remarked, "America, *goniff!*"

Baked Striped Bass Caponata

The Demolished Man was written in our summer cottage out on Fire Island, and I used to relax from the agony of writing by surf-fishing for striped bass and bluefish every dawn and dusk. I well remember the evening on the beach when the idea of using typographical gimmicks for the names of the characters flashed through my mind in the middle of a cast. I reeled in like a maniac, rushed back to the house and began experimenting on the typewriter. People have been kind enough to admire the originality of that novel. I'm proud of that but even prouder of a recipe for striped bass which I invented at the same time and which has had

27

great success with the few friends to whom I've been willing to divulge the secret formula.

1. A three-to-five-pound striped bass (old-timers call them stripe-ed bass), scaled, gutted, washed clean. Remove the fins and gills with heavy shears but leave the head and tail attached. Incidentally, the striped bass, like some forms of fowl, is the better for a little aging. If the fish is quite fresh-caught, a day or two of quiet rest in the fridge improves its flavor tremendously. Of course it must be cleaned first.

2. Stuff the fish, including the head cavity, to the bursting point with a classic poultry dressing well seasoned to your taste. Mine starts with Pepperidge Farm bread stuffing, to which is added: chopped leafy celery tops, finely sliced onion, parsley, basil oregano, ground salt and ground pepper, one or two beaten eggs, melted butter, and a little chicken stock to moisten the dressing so that it will bind and hold. Be sure to mix and knead the dressing with your hands.

3. Use a good French or Italian olive oil to lubricate the bottom of a baking pan. Place the striper in the pan stuffing side down, so that the fish will be erect in its swimming posture. If it has been well crammed with dressing, the dressing itself will serve as a broad base and support for the fish.

4. Now add olive oil to the contents of three or four cans of caponata, which is an Italian *hors d'oeuvre* featuring eggplant and can be bought in almost any good supermarket. Stir until thoroughly mixed and of the consistency of a very thick soup. Spread the mixture over the back of the fish from head to tail. Some of the mixture should be reserved for basting.

5. Sock into a hot preheated oven and let it have twenty minutes at high heat to lock in the flavor. Then open the door for a quick cooling, reduce the temperature to 315° F., close the door and bake for an hour or more, depending on how well done you

like your fish, basting occasionally with the rest of the caponata mix.

Serve whole in the original baking pan, permitting the guests to carve out the parts of the fish they prefer and spooning the caponata sauce onto their plates. A five-pound fish plus the dressing will serve six easily.

Striped Bass Fishballs

When we have a good run of striped bass at Fire Island we sometimes catch more fish than we can eat. This is anathema to the sportsman who insists on eating what he catches. Some fishermen clean and freeze their fish. I'm not of that school; I believe in fishballs of my own devising.

1. Scale, gut, wash, and remove all fins from the bass; the gills, too. Poach very gently in tap water, with seasoning added to form a makeshift court bouillon: celery, onions, carrots, parsley, salt and pepper, thyme, bay leaf.

2. Meanwhile, boil a quantity of white potatoes. Skin them while they're hot and rice them into a bowl. You'll need a ricer for that, but every good kitchen should have one.

3. When the fish is done, take the meat off the bones and mix it half-and-half with the riced potatoes. Taste it as you mix and add whatever seasoning you think it requires.

4. Crunch up a box (large) of cornflakes with your hands and place the crumbs in a large bowl. Shape the fish-potato mix into fishballs about the size of a handball. Roll them in the cornflakes until they're well covered.

Now you can eat them immediately or freeze them for the future. When the time comes to serve, sauté them gently in butter on top of the range or else bake them until they're hot. The court bouillon may be strained through cheesecloth and frozen for future use.

At Fire Island I've learned many lessons about preparing food from the sea. Most people do it an injustice by handling and cooking it too roughly. Seafood is in a class with the omelet, which is also much abused. It must be cooked with tact and exquisite timing, and certainly with concentration. The chef who has a dozen other things on his or her mind is bound to fail.

ANTHONY BOUCHER

Phyllis White writes:

The book sounds enticing and it would be nice to see some Boucher in it along with his friends. I do have many other recipes of his. I am sending along a sampling . . .

[Phyllis White generously sent a dozen recipes and it was one of the hardest jobs ever performed to choose among them. Actually there should *be* an Anthony Boucher Cookbook, something Poul Anderson says "had long been in Tony's mind." — ED.]

Curry De Luxe

1 tbsp curry powder

$\frac{1}{4}$ tsp. anise or fennel

$\frac{1}{4}$ tsp. paprika

$\frac{1}{4}$ tsp. chili powder

$\frac{1}{4}$ tsp. turmeric

$\frac{1}{4}$ tsp. mace

$\frac{1}{4}$ tsp. ground cloves

$\frac{1}{4}$ tsp. cumin

$\frac{1}{8}$ tsp. cardamom

5 tbsp. olive oil ($\frac{1}{3}$ cup)

1 large onion

1 green pepper

1 apple

1 clove garlic

2 tbsp. raisins or chopped dates, optional

1 tbsp. Worcestershire sauce

2 lbs. lean stewing lamb

(more)

31

1 cup boiling water

1 bouillon cube

2 tbsp. tomato paste

1 lime or small lemon

1 tbsp. sherry

1 tbsp. milk

1 egg

Make a powder of the first group of nine ingredients. Grind the whole spices in a mortar, add the others, and mix thoroughly. Chop the vegetables and fruit coarsely and sauté them in the oil with Worcestershire and $\frac{1}{2}$ the powder mixture. Add the meat and brown it with the rest of the powder. Dissolve the bouillon cube and paste in the water and pour over all. Let simmer for $1\frac{1}{4}$ hours. Remove the meat to a serving platter. Add the sherry and the juice of the lime or lemon to the curry in the pan. Beat an egg lightly in the milk, add this, and cook, stirring, about another minute, or until it begins to thicken. Pour over the meat, and serve with rice and chutney. This should serve four, but two can make a terrible hole in it.

Roast Stuffed Turkey

For the record, this is how I cooked my best turkey to date [1942]:

It was a $14\frac{1}{2}$ -pound bird from Corning and I was lucky enough to get some extra heads and feet with it. On the first day I cleaned the bird thoroughly, singed it, singed the heads too, stripped it of fat, and cut out the neck. I put the neck, heads, feet, gizzard, and heart in a soup pot and covered them with cold water, adding vegetable flakes (over a half tin), celery and onion flakes (about 2 tbsp. each), a handful of chopped parsley, a sliced clove of garlic, a tsp. of paprika, a few coriander seeds, some salt, and about $1\frac{1}{2}$ cups of white wine. I brought this to a boil and let it simmer about 2 hrs., adding more water when necessary to cover, and adding the liver halfway through cooking.

Then came the stuffing:

1. In a large bowl (dishpan to be exact) I put about 2 lbs. of bread crumbs (one $1\frac{1}{2}$ lb. loaf toasted and ground plus crumbs on hand). Mix this well with 1 lb. pork sausage. Add about half the rendered turkey fat (with grieven) and $\frac{1}{2}$ lb. Nucoa melted in 2 oz. burned brandy. Mix very well.

2. Chop and mix in a bowl 4 large onions, 4 cloves garlic, a handful parsley, a handful celery tops, 1 can drained water chestnuts, and 2 large apples.

3. Grind in a mortar (where necessary) and mix: 1 tbsp. salt, 1 tbsp. poultry seasoning, 2 tsp. sage, and 1 tsp. each of allspice, caraway seed, celery seed, cumin, mace, marjoram, mustard, oregano, coarse black pepper, rosemary, savory, thyme, and turmeric, and $\frac{1}{2}$ tsp. cayenne.

4. Mix all these three bowls thoroughly and then some more. Stuff the turkey at both ends and put the rest in a baking dish. Run skewers through the tail-gap and lace and skewer the neck-skin back over the neck gap. Insert skewers in the wings and truss the bird.

Second day:

I tried the dough-blanket method, which is a nuisance to prepare but good. I cooked the bird about 4 hrs., adding occasional water. The last hour I put the baking dish of extra dressing into the oven, moistened with stock.

Gravy:

Remove all flesh from necks and heads. Chop giblets. Strain six cups of stock. Add 12 tbsp. ($\frac{3}{4}$ cup) flour to grease and juices in pan (only what I did was first remove those grease-and-juices to a deep roasting pan). Make roux, cook a few minutes, then slowly add stock. When gravy bubbles and thickens, add meat and giblets and cook a few minutes longer. No seasoning necessary except a little salt.

Veal Pot Roast

(Note: The pot roast principle is usually applied only to beef, and hence many people, those who dislike beef unless it bleeds, imagine that they don't like pot roasts. Almost any meat, however, can be served as a pot roast . . .)

4 lbs. veal (shoulder, leg, breast)	2 bay leaves
1 tbsp. salt	2 chili tepines
3 tbsp. flour	3 whole allspice
2 tbsp. bacon grease (or other shortening)	($\frac{1}{2}$ blade mace)
1 onion, sliced	($\frac{3}{4}$ tsp. cumin)
1 clove garlic, chopped	1 cup water
	$\frac{1}{2}$ cup wine vinegar

Mix salt and flour together and dredge the meat thoroughly in this mixture. Melt the shortening in a heavy kettle, Dutch oven, or covered heavy fryer over a high flame. Brown the meat well on all sides. Turn the flame low and add onion, garlic, seasonings, water, and vinegar. Cover and simmer about 3 hours. Add another $\frac{1}{2}$ cup of water as it needs it — about 2 cups more in all. When you remove the finished roast, you'll find that it has made its own gravy, and very good too.

MARION ZIMMER BRADLEY

Breakfast Cookies

1 cup sugar

1 cup unsulphured
molasses (the sweet
kind is better than
blackstrap)

1 cup bacon drippings or
other soft shortening*

1 cup hot black coffee,
strong

2 small eggs

2 tsp. cinnamon

1 tsp. ginger

$\frac{1}{2}$ tsp. nutmeg

$\frac{1}{4}$ tsp. cloves

1 tsp. baking soda in hot
water

$3\frac{1}{2}$ to $4\frac{1}{2}$ cups flour

raisins, optional

Glaze:

1 cup confectioner's sugar thinned with orange juice until
spreadable

*You can use unsalted shortening instead of bacon dripping
but then add 1 tsp. salt. You can substitute water for coffee but
flavor will not be as good. You can also make them conventional
fashion — i.e., mix sugars, shortening, liquid, and egg; then sift
all the spices, flour, soda, and salt together. But I make them this
way.

Mix together in a deep bowl the sugar, molasses, bacon drippings or shortening, coffee. Mix thoroughly, and add two small eggs. To this mixture add the spices. Dissolve one teaspoon of baking soda in hot water and add to mixture; stir lightly.

When the fizzing quiets, stir in, in two or three portions, enough flour to make a soft dough. This would be between $3\frac{1}{2}$ and $4\frac{1}{2}$ cups of flour. Flours vary so much that I cannot be certain. The dough should be a little thicker than cake batter, but certainly softer than most cookie dough: it should flow rather than drop from the spoon when warm.

Chill the dough. Then drop by spoonfuls on a greased cookie sheet, leaving some room for spreading, and bake at 350° F. until just set (i.e., your finger should leave almost no imprint in the top of the test cookie). They will solidify slightly when they cool. However, they should be tender and cakelike: if the first batch seem doughy, or if they bake in rocklike lumps instead of melting down and spreading, there is too much flour in them; thin your batter slightly with coffee before baking the next batch.

These are wonderful as a fairly hearty snack for children. If you prefer, you can stir raisins into them. For tea with the ladies, you can allow them to cool and glaze them lightly with confectioners' sugar (1 cup) thinned with orange juice until spreadable. They are not nearly as rich or sweet as the commercial cookies and are wonderful to dunk in your coffee, or tea, at midmorning brunch.

REGINALD BRETNOR

The first two recipes are variations on recipes for which Charles Krug gave me three bottles of wine apiece; besides, they taste good. The third is, in my opinion, a joy and a delight, and I have never given it to anyone before, though I have served it to several.

I also have a recipe for Moose Bourguignon, with chicken livers, which sounds ominous but is delicious. It starts, roughly, "Take one moose, or x pounds of moosemeat . . ." If you want it, I'll send it along. You will notice that my recipes are deliberately vague. The reason for that is very simple: one general method of cooking fish, if it is sound, can be adapted to any number of varieties of fish; a bouquet garni, as long as one overdoes nothing, can be varied almost infinitely. When cooking with wine, especially when we cook fish, the quality of wine is very important. It is better to cook with fine wine and to drink the cooking sherry than vice versa.

Beef Tongue in Caper Sauce

Surround beef tongue in saucepan with 1 medium carrot, 1 stalk of celery, 1 large onion, all sliced. Add bouquet garni consisting of $\frac{1}{2}$ teaspoon thyme, $\frac{1}{4}$ teaspoon rosemary, 8 crushed peppercorns, $\frac{1}{2}$ teaspoon powdered orange peel, 1 bay leaf. Cover with any dry white wine, any rosé, or a very light red.

Simmer until the tongue is tender enough to skin. Remove

from the pot, skin, and tidy up. Return to pot and simmer until the tongue can be cut with a fork. Then strain three cups of the stock and reduce by about a third. In a double boiler, melt 3 tablespoons of butter and add flour for a smooth roux. Make your sauce, using $\frac{1}{2}$ stock, $\frac{1}{2}$ milk, adding slowly and stirring until smooth. Finally add $1\frac{1}{2}$ tablespoons of capers and 1 teaspoon caper liquid. Slice the tongue and serve with rice, the sauce over both.

Fish Steamed in Wine

A very quick and simple recipe for almost any white fish or for salmon. Pour about $\frac{1}{4}$ of an inch of really good white wine into the bottom of a steamer or a covered saucepan into which you can put a rack. Put over it a pound or more of filet of halibut or sole or salmon or whatever (or, say, a halibut or sea bass steak) and steam until tender — only a few minutes if fileted or sliced, longer if a large section. Reserve the fish. Keep it warm.

Then, in the steamer, make a sauce: Make a roux of one teaspoon (more or less) of flour and butter, add to juice in pan; as you stir add the undrained contents of a 2-ounce can of mushrooms. As the sauce thickens add more wine slowly if necessary, and a pinch ($\frac{1}{4}$ teaspoon or less) of summer savory. Garnish the fish with chopped hardboiled egg, pour the sauce over it, and serve on a warmed platter.

Turkey Drumsticks in Wine

If you can find frozen turkey drumsticks — the bigger the better; those from 20-to-30-lb. birds seem to be the best — thaw them. Then brown them in the hottest oven you can manage — 550°-600° F. is ideal. Put them into a pan where they fit fairly closely; add a dozen or so (if you have four drumsticks) finely chopped green onions (bulbs and stems) and about a cup of sliced fresh mushrooms. Add a bouquet garni — I use thyme, rosemary, a bay leaf, crushed peppercorns, a pinch or two of dried, powdered lemon or orange peel, but this is not rigid; add what you feel is right. Cover with wine. Simmer very slowly until tender. They get *very* tender and really more tasty than chicken. Serve with plain rice or with one of the fancier packaged rice mixes. The sauce: very much as in the beef tongue recipe without the capers.

JOHN BRUNNER

Over the last decade or so we've gradually evolved the following menu, which Marjorie cooks two or three times a year for our guests because it boasts numerous advantages — it's delicious, it's varied, it's surprisingly inexpensive, and it's elastic so that it can be stretched or shrunk to meet the occasion. Quantities are given for 4-6; we don't generally like to attempt big dinner parties because we feel that six at table is the maximum number which gives us a chance to talk at reasonable length with everybody.

Before dinner we offer sherry as an *aperitif*, a choice of dry or medium-sweet, together with peanuts *à la Grecque* (oven roasted with coarse salt), and/or *arare* (Japanese rice-crackers with seaweed in them), and/or "Indian nosh" (something we've never found out the proper name for because the sort of shop where you get it is likely to have a proprietor who can only spell it in Devangri script), which you may identify when I say that it consists of nuts mixed with strands, balls, and lumps of something crisp and yellow, delicately spiced.

We never serve hard liquor before dinner, since we concur with the French view that too much alcohol dulls the palate. But equally suitable would be any of the well-known, and some of the not-so-well-known, *aperitif* drinks: dry vermouth, St. Raphael, Campari, Cynar, or what-have-you.

Then we adjourn to the table and begin the proceedings with . . .

Cold Borscht

1 lb. uncooked beetroot (beets)	2 pts. meat stock
$\frac{1}{2}$ lb. onions	butter
1 leek	salt, pepper, brown sugar
2 cloves garlic	vinegar
	sour cream

Prepare the meat stock (Marjorie makes her own from assorted bones). Chop onions, garlic, and leek very fine. Cook in minimum amount of butter over low heat until soft. Add beetroot, peeled and diced. Season with salt, pepper, a dash of vinegar, and enough brown sugar to kill the excessive sharpness of the latter (try 1 tsp. of each to begin with, adjust to taste). Pour stock over and simmer until color has gone from beetroot — about two hours. Strain, allow to cool, and serve with sour cream to be dolloped into the middle of each plateful. Hard breadsticks.

With this and the following course we generally finish our sherry and switch to a dry white wine, slightly chilled. The following course is, in fact . . .

Squid With Pine Nuts

1 lb. baby squid	1 clove garlic
1 large onion	salt and pepper
1 oz. pine nuts (pinon nuts)	2 sherry-glasses dry sherry
2 oz. butter	water

Chop the onion and garlic fine, brown in the butter. Clean squid, cut into rings, add to pan and add nuts. Season lightly. Stir over low heat until everything is coated with the butter. Add the sherry. Simmer for 2-3 minutes. Add water to barely cover. Simmer until squid is tender — approximately 20 minutes, but this depends on the age of the squid: the older, the longer. Serve hot. Keep the breadsticks coming.

Try and finish off the white wine at the same time the last bit of squid disappears. (It will. I've seen people who were convinced they didn't like the stuff come back for seconds of this dish, then ask optimistically for thirds — too late.)

Then we get down to the really serious item on the agenda, a member of that family of classic peasant dishes which runs from Normandy to Yugoslavia and can probably be found in recognizable form in the New World, too. What they amount to, basically, is a means of making stored beans taste wonderful when that's all you've got for a large family. Any number of changes can be rung on the fundamental principle. Here's Marjorie's personal version of a . . .

Cassoulet à la Normandie

1 lb. beans (haricot, black-eyed, kidney, or red are all suitable but hard beans must be soaked overnight while black-eyed need be soaked only for an hour or two)

$\frac{1}{2}$ lb. onions, chopped fine

1 clove garlic, ditto

1 lb. tomatoes, peeled and sliced

4 oz. bacon cut in small squares or strips

$\frac{1}{2}$ lb. sliced garlic sausage

1 lb. pork chipolata sausages

(more)

1 small chicken, jointed
(or equivalent
quantity of duck,
turkey, goose, pigeon)

bouquet garni

salt and pepper

1 cup dry white wine

chicken stock

2 oz. butter

breadcrumbs

Simmer beans in advance until nearly but not quite tender. Melt bacon in butter, add chopped onions, garlic, tomato and leave to keep warm on low heat — the mixture must blend but not dry up. Meantime put the bouquet garni in the bottom of a large casserole. Distribute the chicken around and over it. Lay the chipolata sausages over the chicken and spread the garlic sausage over that. Season. Add wine. Strain the beans and cover the chicken, etc., with a deep layer of them. Spread over the beans the bacon-onion-tomato-garlic mixture. Wash it in, gently pouring on stock to raise liquid level to about $\frac{2}{3}$ of the way up the layer of beans (this is why we use a Pyrex casserole for choice!), and cover with breadcrumbs to help keep the steam in. Cook without a lid in a moderate oven (Regulo 4, 375° F.) for about 2 hours. Serve with an *assiette de crudités* or a plain green salad, eaten off sideplates because otherwise the liquid from the cassoulet will make it soggy.

With a tough peasant dish like this you need a tough peasant wine. Go for a fat brutal Burgundy of the kind that marches down your throat with big muddy boots rather than a delicate Bordeaux, which would be wasted. But any substantial red will do — in fact one of the best we've ever found was a wine from the Greek island of Samos. At this stage we tend to do a disgraceful thing and finish the bottle with an intervening cigarette, but most people seem to need a break before the final item, to whit . . .

Baked Bananas

1 banana per person, halved and sliced lengthwise

orange and lemon juice

nutmeg and cinnamon

brown sugar and clear honey

unsalted butter

dark rum

Lay bananas in a baking dish. Sprinkle with spices and sugar. Trickle over 1 tsp. clear honey. Pour over juice of 1 orange and $\frac{1}{2}$ lemon (proportionately to the number of bananas — the eventual sauce should be thick and syrupy so don't overdo it) and a sherryglassful of dark rum. Dot with shavings of butter. Bake in moderate oven for about 30 minutes. Serve hot.

And for those people who still have a trace of appetite left, we wind up with a cheeseboard, a dish of grapes, and a bowl of those spongy English sweets called marshmallows. If one must have a wine with this course, it had better be either an out-and-out dessert wine (a very sweet port, a Marsala, sweet Madeira, sweet sherry, Commandaria, or such-like), or a sweet sparkling wine. More likely, however, we will retire to the drawing room for coffee and a glass of liqueur.

Some minor additional comments. The borscht can be made the day before; what's more, if you use yeast extract for the stock instead of bones, you turn it into an excellent vegetarian soup, which has delighted our friends of that persuasion. The squid recipe works equally well for octopus (or cuttlefish or inkfish or whatever name they apply in your neck of the woods) and doesn't suffer in the least from being cooked earlier and warmed through directly before serving. Surprisingly, though it isn't in the least Chinese, it makes a highly compatible dish at a Chinese meal. In that case, you can add a dash of soy sauce, but it's not required. You can even try an elaboration which came to me in a flash of inspiration one time when we had more people than we expected for dinner: proceed exactly as described, then pile the squid on a layer of that luscious black Chinese seaweed and pour the liquid over. It worked a treat. Don't forget to "develop" and cook the seaweed first. The bananas can be prepared and put in the oven under the cassoulet, then kept warm while you're eating the latter.

As to sources . . . well, no doubt the basic idea for each of these dishes came from *somewhere*, but after ten or more years they've evolved to the point where no amount of research in Marjorie's extensive library of cookbooks will enable us to locate identical recipes. Ultimately the borscht is probably Polish rather than Russian (it may be Ukrainian), but it's become highly personalized. The squid recipe is certainly Mediterranean in origin, and those pine nuts would suggest Northern Italy; here again, though, emendation, adaptation, and variation have ensued. The cassoulet, as indicated, is of the Norman type, but it's the kind of dish you can alter in countless ways without affecting its underlying nature — as far as we can make out, the recipe we began with was one which called for "a leg and a wing from a smoked goose"! And one suspects that the baked bananas are West Indian. What's described here is the best version we've found after testing a wide range of alternatives.

Variation, of course, has its limits. We do *not* believe that you can fill a dish with salami and polenta and call the result toad-in-the-hole!

Some Bachelor Type Recipes

If I had to cook ever day I'd hate it. Luckily, I only have to cook when I feel like it, and consequently I rather enjoy turning out quick snack-type items. In fact, I've devised some myself.

They almost always include those old bachelor standbys, eggs and cheese. Here's one which I recall cooking in Kate and Damon Knight's kitchen on the only occasion when I attended a Milford SF Writer's Conference . . .

Scrambled Eggs à la Brunner

about 2 large eggs per person (less for breakfast, e.g., 7 eggs for four people; more for brunch, e.g., 10 eggs for four people)

milk

toast

butter

Parmesan cheese

soy sauce or mushroom ketchup or garlic salt

fresh-ground black pepper and sea salt, if possible

a few chopped chives if liked

Take a heavy saucepan with a well-fitting lid. Set the pan on a medium heat and for each egg put in approximately 1 dessert-spoonful milk and a shaving of butter. Meantime put toast to brown. As soon as the butter starts to melt but before the milk can boil, break in the eggs and stir with a wooden spoon or spatula sufficiently to distribute yolk and white evenly. Do not beat or whisk! Turn the heat down to low. Add salt, pepper, a few drops of soy sauce or mushroom ketchup; alternatively, substitute a pinch of garlic salt for some of the regular salt. If liked, add a sprinkle of fresh chives, spring onion green, or scallion green. Keep the mixture moving gently: if you let it dry on the bottom of the pan, it will stick (says Marjorie) worse than burnt porridge. As and when you can, lightly butter the toast — don't try buttering more than one slice without going back to the pan for another stir — and dredge it with a little grated Parmesan. When the last white-of-egg is about to turn from transparent to white, remove from heat and put the lid on. The whole art of making these eggs come out right lies in allowing them to set rather than cook through. After 2-3 minutes pile on toast and serve. They should be moist but not wet. If they're dry, don't bother eating them. Start again.

I served the foregoing to a Turkish SF fan who had just suggested, at 2 A.M., that we go out for a gourmet meal. London is a fine town, but my idea of a gourmet meal is not to be found in the establishments open there at that time of the morning, such as Wimpy bars. So I fixed scrambled eggs as above and I think he was fairly well satisfied.

As to the following: well, our friends Pierre and Tania Vandenberghe, who run Belgium's only specialist SF bookstore, are vegetarians and were understandably suspicious when I offered to introduce them to *le lapin du Pays de Galles*. A few months later, however, when we saw them again in Brussels, I learned that they were buying Cheddar cheese from a shop specializing in imported delicacies purely in order to let it dry up and go hard enough to make a good . . .

Welsh Rabbit

toast

hard dry cheese
(Cheddar is best, but
any that doesn't go
stringy when melted
will do — Red
Leicester is also very
successful.)

something to sharpen it:
dry mustard, English
mustard, French
mustard, horseradish
cream . . .

something to moisten it:
milk or beer

47

Okay, this is not 100 percent authentic, but basically a Welsh rabbit (not, please, rarebit!) is a way of making bread and cheese into a substantial dish.

Grate the cheese into big coarse flakes, about 3 tsp. per slice of toast. Add the sharpening. Add sufficient liquid to coat the cheese thoroughly with the sharpening. Spread in an even layer over toast and set under a low grill until completely melted, then turn up the heat to brown the top.

If you put a poached egg on top of a regular Welsh rabbit, that turns it into a buck rabbit.

Kids like the pretty color you get by using tomato ketchup (no liquid) instead of mustard. And an astonishingly good snack can be made by laying pigs of orange or tangerine and thin slices of raw unpeeled apple on the toast before covering with cheese. (I invented that myself and never bothered to give it a name.)

Speaking of things I invented myself: I don't know whether it was due to my Swiss ancestry, but I compiled the following from what happened to be in the fridge one Sunday morning, and it wasn't until years later that I realized I'd recreated the *Bauernomelette*. Unrepentantly, I continue to cook it *my* way and to call it . . .

Eggy Mess

butter	left-over potato (or sweet potato), if any
onion(s)	
mushrooms	a banana, preferably underripe
bacon	
soy sauce, salt, garlic salt, pepper or red pepper	about 3 eggs for two people

The beauty of this is that each ingredient requires about as much more cooking time than its successor as the latter takes to be ready for the pan.

Throw a walnut-sized lump of butter into a skillet and melt it over low heat while peeling and slicing an onion or 2-3 shallots. Put in the onion and stir around. Peel and slice the mushrooms. Add them and stir. Cut up the bacon with scissors into odd bits; add that and stir. If you have any cold boiled potatoes, or sweet potatoes, or anything, by all means add that too. Finally peel and slice a banana and add that. Break your eggs into a bowl, season them, and for each add 1 tsp. cold water (this, by the way, is the trick that makes omelets of any kind work). Beat the eggs as though they'd done you an injury. By that time the banana will show signs of going squidgy. Turn up the heat and at once pour in the eggs. Draw the mixture away from the sides of the pan to let the uncooked part run under in normal omelette fashion. Fold and serve.

EDWARD BRYANT

. . . my own favorite way of gaining weight, but healthily:

Granola Nisbet

2 cups whole wheat flour

3 cups rolled oats

1 cup soya flour

1 cup wheat germ

1 cup millet

$1\frac{1}{2}$ cups honey

3 or 4 cups walnuts, chopped

1 cup hulled sunflower seeds

$\frac{1}{2}$ cup sesame seeds

1 cup coconut

1 cup oil

1 cup water

Combine dry ingredients. Add water, oil, and honey, one at a time. Crumble onto 2 cookie sheets. Bake at 350° F. Stir often until golden (20-30 minutes).

Serve for breakfast or anytime for a snack. Eat plain or as cereal with milk, brown sugar, etc.

DORIS PITKIN BUCK

Rice with Eggs

$1\frac{1}{3}$ cups Minute Rice
salt
1 pat butter
2 eggs

black pepper, fresh
ground
chili powder, optional

Prepare Minute Rice for four (according to directions on package). When done, stir in 2 eggs.

The heat of the rice cooks them to creaminess.

In any case, use plenty of black pepper at the end. If you like chili powder, stir that in too.

Yield: a filling supper for two.

Preparation time: 7 minutes.

I used this long before Minute Rice was invented.

KENNETH BULMER

Pamela Bulmer writes:

Yorkshire Pudding

The trouble with favorite recipes is that one cooks them automatically, using one's own quick measuring or weighing utensils. When asked to write it down, one has to work it out precisely, find the original you adapted from or the dog-eared 20-year-old scrap of paper.

I arrived home [in England] to find that my 16-year-old babysitter, an excellent little cook, had had a hard time living up to my reputation, heavily exaggerated by the children!

This one is included for the sake of the anecdote, which I think deserved preserving:

Yorkshire pudding is not so much a recipe as a national institution which gives the lie to the tale about bad British cooking. Some years ago Ken and I were the guests of American fandom and were staying with Doc Barrett and his family at Indian Lake. The fame of York*shyre* Pudding had already spread to Ohio and I was at length prevailed upon to make a real one to satisfy both the Barrett appetite and their curiosity. Zero hour approached and I asked for the first ingredient — $\frac{1}{2}$ oz. of dripping. "$\frac{1}{2}$ oz. of *what*?" came the stunned reply. "$\frac{1}{2}$ oz. of dripping — the meat juices and fat from roast beef." "Oh, you mean the grease!" (I shuddered.) "We tip that in the garbage."

If that's what you call it, I can't say I blame them. I settled for $\frac{1}{2}$ oz. of colorless, tasteless lard and shocked my hosts still further by explaining that we spread dripping, together with jellied meat juices, on toast with salt and pepper for a quick snack or fry bread in it, to say nothing of the delights of bubble and squeak — cooked cabbage, potatoes, and onions mixed together and fried. Scrumptious — and all three especially beloved in the working classes and a dead giveaway for a non-class, non-snob person. To continue, I made the Yorkshire Pudding, having carefully timed the operation so that it would be ready to serve immediately. Only as I went to take it out of the oven did I realize that a barbecue was planned and this would be served at the bottom of the garden. Yorkshire Puddings are rather like soufflés — they don't like draughts and they don't like hanging about. There was nothing for it but to sprint. My creation had risen superbly for the occasion, like a mock pregnancy, and I must hold the world record for Yorkshire Pudding Sprinters. Everyone was seated, waiting to be served, when I placed my offering triumphantly on the table. Worse was to come. I was completely out of breath and therefore speechless, and watched with mounting horror as the dish was passed from hand to hand and subjected to the most intense scrutiny, as if it were a dead cockroach. I gasped out that it didn't perform, it should be eaten hot, straight from the oven with gravy, roast beef, and roast potatoes. Before my eyes it shrank until all that remained was a tired, deflated, cardboard-colored lump. It just died from that indignity. It was a culinary disaster ranking with the time I made meringue with salt.

For the record:

4 oz. flour	1 egg
$\frac{1}{2}$ pt. milk or milk and water	good pinch salt
	dripping

Sift dry ingredients, make a well in the center, break in the egg and beat gradually, adding the milk, until mixture looks like smooth cream. Alternatively, blend at maximum speed in a liquidizer. Leave to stand for about 1 hour. Heat about $\frac{1}{2}$ oz. dripping in a baking tin until *very hot*. Beat the batter again until bubbles appear on the surface, then pour into tin and bake in hot oven (400° F.) for about 30 minutes. The amount of time and dripping will vary slightly according to the size of the tin — mine is about 10 inches square. If using individual patty tins, it will take about 10 minutes.

There are countless variations. Here are a few:

Heat sausages for ten minutes, then add batter; cook as before. Ditto for lamb chops.

As a dessert, use two eggs and substitute butter for dripping. Slice 1 lb. cooking apples, add a few crushed coriander seeds, heat thoroughly in oven, then add batter as before. Some dried fruit can also be added to the batter, if liked. Serve hot with melted butter and dredge with castor sugar.

Or chop up 1 lb. rhubarb, add ginger to taste, and proceed as before.

Bacon in Bulmer Sauce

$3\frac{1}{2}$-to-4-lb. joint of lean bacon or ham

a couple of carrots, onions, and some sticks of celery (or celery salt)

a good pinch of cinnamon

a few cloves

Bulmer's cider to cover

For the Sauce:

$\frac{1}{2}$ pt. stock	1 oz. brown sugar
pepper	4 oz. seedless raisins
juice of $\frac{1}{2}$ lemon	1 rounded tsp. cornflour

Method:

Soak joint overnight to remove excess salt. Place joint with first set of ingredients in a pan to fit. If pan is too large, you will need a great deal of cider. Cover and simmer, allowing 20 minutes to the pound. If using pressure cooker, time according to your instructions, and reduce liquid to about 1 pt.

When joint is cooked, strain off $\frac{1}{2}$ pt. stock. If your joint was not very lean you will have to skim off the excess fat carefully. Strain the stock. I prefer to liquidize mine, and then straining is unnecessary. Place the raisins, stock, sugar, lemon juice, and pepper in a saucepan and simmer about 10 minutes. Blend the cornflour with a little cold water, add to the sauce, and cook until it thickens.

Serve with patna rice, and vegetables of choice. Our favorites are runner or French beans and sweet corn. Serve the sauce separately.

I sometimes substitute beer for the cider, which gives a darker color to the meat. Half cider or beer and water can also be used. Red or white wine is also very successful.

Blackberry Crisp Ambrosia

1 lb. blackberries

juice and grated rind of 1 lemon

2 eggs

1 cup brown breadcrumbs

1 cup desiccated coconut

1 oz. butter

2 oz. sugar

2 oz. chopped nuts

$\frac{1}{4}$ pt. whipped cream

Reserve a few blackberries for decoration. Cook the rest with the lemon rind and juice gently until soft, then pass through a strainer to remove seeds. Beat eggs and stir in. Cook until mixture thickens, but *do not boil*. Allow to cool.

Melt the butter and add breadcrumbs, coconut, and sugar and place in oven until crisp. Stir occasionally, and be careful not to burn.

Place a layer of crumb mixture, then blackberry alternately until serving dish is full, finishing with crumbs. Whip the cream, pile on the top, and decorate with the chopped nuts and blackberries. It is best to delay combining the crumb and blackberry mixture until shortly before serving so that the crumbs and coconut remain crisp.

Malt Loaf

8 oz. flour

1 egg

pinch salt

$\frac{1}{2}$ cup sultanas (raisins)

1 small tsp. bi-carb.

1 tbsp. malt extract

1 cup milk

2 tbsp. Golden Syrup (Lyons' — a British import, not always obtainable. Alternative suggestion from editor — try molasses.)

2 tsp. sugar (pref. brown)

Warm malt, milk, and syrup in saucepan. Meanwhile, sieve all dry ingredients in basin together. Remove mixture in pan from heat when melted, stir, and allow to cool for a few minutes. Add to dry ingredients and mix to a soft dough. Pour into greased 1-lb. loaf tin and bake in moderately hot oven for 1 hour. It can be sliced and buttered, but is very good without the butter.

I first made this when I was 12 years old. It's simple and quick, a good standby, and has never let me down. My eldest daughter has just started making it.

GRANT CARRINGTON

Spam Chowder

This recipe is very useful for struggling young writers, artists, folksingers, hippies, or computer-programmers-on-welfare. I can't give you precise details, but it shouldn't be too hard to figure out. One of my old girlfriends used to make it for me, and it's really great to come out of a cold snowy street to find a hot spicy bowl of Spam Chowder waiting for you.

I guess it's made the same way Clam Chowder is made, only with Spam. And hence, much cheaper: First, get a bag of frozen mixed vegetables from your local supermarket. (Or grow, pick, and mix them yourself if you're thusly inclined.) Add lots of milk, and butter, and whatever else goes into Clam Chowder (except clams, which are expensive). Be sure to add lots of pepper and spices, because it helps kill the Spam taste. And, of course, add Spam, diced into little pieces. How long you cook it (boil it? stew it?) I don't know, but I don't think an experienced cook would have much trouble.

1 package frozen mixed vegetables	2 tbsp. flour
1 chopped onion	1 can Spam, in tiny pieces
1 quart milk	salt, pepper to taste
2 tbsp. butter	other spices optional

Melt butter in large saucepan, add flour and stir until thick. Then slowly add milk until white sauce is smooth. Salt, pepper, and season to taste. Then dump in chopped onion, the frozen vegetables, and diced Spam. Simmer slowly for twenty minutes. Can be reheated and tastes the better for "aging." Leave it covered on the stove for instant heating when you stumble in out of freezing weather . . . just the thing for Irish winters.

THEODORE COGSWELL

(I'm in class giving a test. What there will be of this will be jerky because I have to look up at thirty-second intervals to try and discourage my F students from copying from each other.)

Lentil Soup

1. Big pot, water.
2. Ham bone, or ham, or bacon, or salt pork (in small cubes).
3. Lentils.
4. Boil like hell.
5. When helled add chopped cabbage, onions, potatoes, anything.
6. Simmer.
7. Smoosh up lentils with a whip or masher.
8. Simmer (burns easily — be careful).
9. Someplace along the line add garlic, chili, curry, and anything else that strikes your fancy.
10. Is best when quite thick. If you get tired of stirring, toss the pan in a low oven.
11. Only not too thick. Spoon thick, not fork thick.

P.S. Anytime you're cooking anything, throw some brown sugar in. Does amazing things.

JUANITA COULSON

Sweet and Sour Beef

$\frac{3}{4}$ lb. lean beef (round
   steak is good)

211-size can pineapple
   tidbits

5-oz. can water chestnuts

small jar of pimentos

3-oz. can of button
   mushrooms

Slice meat in fairly thin slivers. Brown. Drain.

Reserve $\frac{1}{4}$ cup pineapple juice. (Drink the remainder as an appetizer.)

Drain and slice water chestnuts.

Drain pimentos. If very large, cut in smaller pieces.

Drain mushrooms. Slice if you wish.

Mix in small jar with lid:

$\frac{1}{4}$ cup vinegar

1 tbsp. cornstarch

$\frac{1}{4}$ cup sugar

$\frac{1}{4}$ cup pineapple juice

Chinese bead molasses
to taste

Add pineapple, water chestnuts, pimentos, and mushrooms to meat.

Shake thickening in jar till smooth; immediately add to meat and vegetable mixture.

Stir until thickened. Serve immediately. May be served over rice or chow mein noodles or as is.

Party Biscuits

2 cups flour

$\frac{1}{2}$ tsp. salt

2 tsp. sugar

4 tsp. baking powder

$\frac{1}{2}$ tsp. cream of tartar

$\frac{1}{2}$ cup shortening

$\frac{1}{3}$ cup milk

Stir together dry ingredients. No particular need to sift with new flour.

Cut in $\frac{1}{2}$ cup shortening until shortening is the size of small peas.

Add *all at once* $\frac{2}{3}$ cup of milk.

Stir with fork until mixture "cleans the bowl."

Turn out on floured board, roll to $\frac{1}{3}$ to $\frac{1}{2}$ inch thick, cut.

Bake on ungreased pan in 450° F. oven for 10 to 12 minutes.

These are delicate biscuits. They should *not* be baked until brown on top. Just the palest golden tinge usually means they're done. And some people like them slightly underdone.

French Fried Onion Batter

1 cup flour

$\frac{1}{2}$ tsp. salt

2 eggs slightly beaten

1 cup milk

1 tbsp. cooking oil

This is a very thick, very clinging batter. It will also keep in the refrigerator. To add character, soak the sliced onion rings in the milk before adding it to the batter.

JACK M. DANN

Real Old-Fashioned Bread Pudding from Brooklyn

1 loaf dry or stale bread
  (my mother uses
  stale)

3 eggs

$\frac{1}{4}$ tsp. salt

$\frac{1}{4}$ tsp. nutmeg

$\frac{1}{2}$ tsp. cinnamon (or more
  to taste)

1 cup sugar (or more to
  taste)

$\frac{1}{2}$ tsp. vanilla (or more)

3 or 4 large apples
  (preferably Northern
  Spys)

$1\frac{1}{3}$ cups milk

$\frac{1}{3}$ cup water and $\frac{1}{2}$ to 1
  cup water

vegetable shortening

Mix eggs, sugar, vanilla, salt, spices, milk, and $\frac{1}{3}$ cup water until all is mixed well. In another large bowl, soak bread in about $\frac{1}{2}$ to 1 cup water and squeeze water out immediately. Then add mixture to bread and mix well again. Peel apples and grate into mixture. Generously grease a large round baking pan (approximately 3-qt. size) with vegetable shortening. Pour mixture into the greased pan and dot with remaining shortening. Bake at 350° F. for $1\frac{1}{2}$ hours or until cake tester comes out clean. Test after one hour.

For variation, raisins may be added to the mixture before baking. Soak them before adding them.

AVRAM DAVIDSON

Old Prospector's Style Coffee
(or, an Example of the Kind of Recipe I
Personally Feel I Can Do Without Just Fine)

Take one pound of coffee beans and roast gently on an old waffle iron. Place roasted beans gently in an old gunny sack and crack gently with ball-peen hammer. Place one handful gently in shallow crock, cover gently with saucepan of pure spring water, leave in sun for three days. Gently strain the liquor through an old bandanna handkerchief, add one bootful of some more spring water (pure), warm up as desired. Never bring to boil. Puke gently after drinking.

Contributed gently for our own pure fun and amusement and as evidence that I have not gone totally off my rocker despite ample opportunity.

Peasant Soup or Peasant Pottage

In a very large pot place such items as beef shanks, beef knuckles, one cow-foot or calf-foot, all sliced by the butcher. Some beef neck bones and some mutton or lamb with the bone. Mutton or lamb preferably lean. A slice of veal is excellent.

Fill pot with water. Have your flame very low. Garlic to taste — my taste would be at least one plump clove of garlic cut up, or equivalent in powder. Salt and pepper of course, and I regard dill (pref. weed if fresh not available) as essential, and I always include basil and rosemary and marjoram. Some oregano isn't bad. Cook for four hours.

Then add one soup chicken, sometimes called a stewing hen, though a rooster should do as well. Include as many fowlsfeet as you can get, if you can get any: scald these a while in boiling water (not in the soup, though, as they tend to be dirty) and make incisions with a sharp knife so as cleanly to peel off the scaly feetskin. Discard skin. Feet into soup. These fowlsfeet are really a first-rate addition. Cook soup for four more hours on same small flame.

Now remove from fire and remove contents from pot and put in another pot or bowl or what-have-you. Put everything in the icebox overnight. In the morning the fat has risen and solidified. Remove it by running knifeblade around sides of pot and then scoring fat like pie pieces. Return meats to soup and soup to fire.

Put water on to boil apartly. Now add what vegetables and tubers you like. I like onions, leeks, potatoes, go easy on carrots and parsnips. If you wish you may make a roux or *einbrenn*: Put some of the fat in a pan and melt. Add some diced onion, brown; remove onion and place in soup. Add a spoon of flour and brown very brown. Add hot soup to make a paste. Dissolve paste in soup pot. Vegetables can cook, say, two hours.

During this while, taste the soup, which will have cooked down. If it is too sticky or stocky, reconstitute it by adding boiling water: cold water retards cooking.

On this soup or pottage, you can go 40 days and nights.

65

GORDON R. DICKSON

Emergency Paté

1 lb. *good* liverwurst
½ lb. cream cheese
½ cup raw mushrooms,
   chopped
1 garlic clove (or touch
   onion powder)

2 oz. scotch whiskey
   (any whiskey or
   brandy, if necessary,
   but *no* other type of
   liquor)

Crush garlic clove (if you're using garlic).

Combine all ingredients except seasoning and whiskey.

Add seasoning.

Beat and mix together, using whiskey to soften mixture until it is all used up.

Form into a loaf, put in refrigerator — if possible, let sit and season for a couple of hours. The longer it sits the better the flavors will mix.

Serve with thin slices, lightly buttered, of pumpernickel or other dark bread. Let guests help themselves from paté loaf.

Dry Sack or any good amontillado sherry goes well with this, although it is rich enough to stand up to mixed drinks. If you have a large or elaborate dinner coming, don't let the guests fill up too much on this paté. They can burn up a chunk of good appetite on it.

N.B. This paté also, by itself, makes an excellent after-theater, after-football-game (night-sort) type of snack. As appetizer, figure above to feed 15-20 persons, depending on age and appetites. As a late snack, with no other food, figure it to handle a half to a third of that number, again depending on appetite. A good late-night accompaniment is champagne (at least to begin with, while the eating's going on). If it's been an evening with food and drink earlier, don't waste a really good champagne. Or pull the host's Sneaky Trick No. 2 — open a bottle of Korbel (the natural, not the brut or extra dry) for the first glass-filling, and then follow with anything in a bottle marked Champagne. Those who want to go beyond this can go to whatever they want in mixed drinks or beer (but stay away from other wine).

Beef Short Ribs with Egg Noodles (or whatever)

short ribs (approx. 1 to $1\frac{1}{2}$ pounds per person)

1 medium-sized onion

mushrooms (to suit the individual preference)

$\frac{1}{2}$ cup red wine (a Bordeaux-type which is a little bit over the hill for drinking purposes is excellent. Otherwise, any stout red — *Hearty Burgundy* by Gallo is interesting)

butter

flour (for roux, with butter)

bay leaf, salt, pepper, etc.

Simmer short ribs, cut into short chunks, in water with bay leaf, some salt, and half of the onion, chopped coarsely.

When the meat on the short ribs is rag-tender, take the ribs out; set stock aside to cool.

Slice other half of onion, fry in butter until transparent, add mushrooms, fry. Add stock (reduce, if necessary, to about a cupful by simmering down) and red wine. Simmer lightly together for a couple of minutes. Make and add roux as necessary to thicken.

Add meat to sauce/gravy.

Serve on noodles (or toast, or potato, or rice . . .)

N.B. You can also go to the trouble of taking the meat off the bones (this looks better at small dinners for two to five people). Taste the resulting meat/sauce *at serving temperature*. If taste is not sufficiently striking to palate, you can help by adding (a) a *little* melted butter (tasting as you add), (b) a *very little* amount of granulated sugar, adding literally a few grains at a time and tasting as you go (properly done, this will make the sauce/gravy taste, not sweeter, but more rich). But if you doubt yourself at all as a cook/taster, don't risk trying either the extra butter or sugar. Both are risky, the sugar damnably so.

THOMAS M. DISCH

By all means, you're welcome to "Invitation." (When have I ever refused anyone a poem!) I'd like to be able to send something extremely typical. Last night I made a decent Eggplant Parmigian', but it's the recipe I learned in New York, and done from memory at that. The spices weren't precise. I do fine stuffings but they're instinctive (I'm bragging). There's one recipe I have in print, however: it's at the end of a story called "5 Eggs" in *Orbit 1*, for a (rather gigantic) Caesar Salad. You're certainly welcome to that, though Caesar Salads are not the rarities today I thought they were in my youth. Ah, but I recall three recipes Charlie and I have done. They're unusual, yet simple.

Beesting

Only cows can make beesting. It's the super-enriched milk that comes out in advance of the regular milk after a cow's given birth. If you put it just as it is into a very low oven overnight, it turns into a kind of custard. This I found out living on a dairy farm in Surrey. It didn't taste like much, but it was free. It was probably very healthy.

Liver and Onions

To my mind this is the only way liver can be made a pleasure rather than an occasional duty. Fill the bottom of a Dutch oven with slices of onion cut rather thick. Put pats of butter on the onions, and just enough water to cover the slices. Let this cook, covered, in a 350° F. oven for half an hour. Meanwhile, dredge the liver, either beef or calf, in a mixture of flour, salt, and pepper. Place the liver on the cooking onions and, still covered, cook for another half hour. Then cook for ten minutes uncovered. The liver becomes very soft and tasty. (In fact, the recipe was invented for geriatric nursing.) Oh — a bay leaf on top of the liver, and coarsely ground thyme in the flour.

Baked Pumpkin

I tried this once, for company, and it was a disaster. The theory is very simple: Scoop out a pumpkin and fill it with sweetened milk. I used sugar; Shakers would have used maple syrup. Also whatever spices you're partial to: cinnamon, nutmeg, ginger, or allspice. Put the top back on and bake it for five hours at a very low temperature — 200° F. This is supposed to take place in a brick oven, however. Don't do what I did: put the pumpkin on a rack; the pumpkin sort of sank through it. It tasted terrible, but I'll probably try it again someday anyhow. It *sounds* like it should be delicious.

Shaker Spinach

Ideally, use fresh spinach, though frozen will do. The water it's boiled in should contain an onion, chopped very fine, and rosemary — if fresh, just two or three leaves; if dried and powdered, an eighth of a teaspoon. I also add a slice of bacon while it cooks, but that's unorthodox.

SONYA DORMAN

Stale Bread is Not for the Birds' Breakfast

Break 6 or 8 slices of stale bread into one- or two-inch pieces. Put them in a bowl, cover with hot water, soak for one minute; then pour off water.

Beat two eggs with some salt and a little milk, pour mixture over bread in bowl, and let stand while you heat a large piece of butter in your skillet.

When the butter is crackling and almost brown, pour in the soaked bread mixture. Keep turning and turning the mixture in the pan until the pieces brown and begin to separate.

Serve with maple syrup or honey. Fried ham or bacon goes very well with this.

Barbequed Veal Ribs

If you're going to have veal ribs for dinner, take out a big pot before lunch, place the veal ribs in the pot, cover with cold water, and simmer for 15 minutes.

Remove ribs, drain them, and place them flat in a large teflon pan. Pour over them the following sauce (all mixed together):

$\frac{1}{2}$ cup teriyaki or soy sauce

1 cup orange juice

2 tsp. brown sugar

Put the panful of ribs and sauce in the fridge. About once an hour you will take the pan out, turn the ribs over, and make sure they are marinating well.

Two hours before serving time, put the pan of ribs into the oven, at 350° F. Baste them with the sauce about every half hour. They will slowly become brown and sticky as the sauce gets thicker and begins to disappear.

When they are dark and sticky, they are ready to serve. Good with rice and a crisp salad.

Curried Lamb Shanks

If your dinner guests are hearty eaters, you'll want to provide two shanks per person.

Lay the shanks out on the counter and rub them well with salt, Madras curry, and some powdered ginger. Then put them into the big teflon pan, or a covered roasting pan. Add to them, tucked in all around, cut carrots and potatoes in medium pieces, and at least one onion, sliced fairly thin. Sprinkle the vegetables with pepper and salt. One package of frozen lima beans may be added. If you don't use a covered roasting pan, cover your teflon pan tightly with aluminum foil.

Roast the shanks at 350° F. in the oven at least two hours. If you decide on another martini before dinner, an extra half hour will do the shanks no harm at all.

Boozer's Dessert

$\frac{1}{2}$ cup light rum

3-oz. package raspberry Jell-O

$\frac{1}{2}$ pint heavy cream

Mix one package of raspberry Jell-O with one cup of boiling water in large bowl until Jell-O is dissolved. Add one-half cup cold water and one-half cup light rum. Put in fridge to cool. Don't let it set.

Beat one-half pint of heavy cream until quite thick but not in peaks. Add to cooled but still-liquid Jell-O and rum, beating it in until moderately well mixed. Turn into separate serving dishes or into a dessert bowl (a glass bowl is pretty) and chill two or three hours until set. This is especially good with macaroons or almond cookies. It will serve three Boozers or four Judges.

GEORGE ALEC EFFINGER

Piglet's Ginger Peachy Soup

32-oz. can peach halves

2 tbsp. cornstarch

1 tbsp. melted butter

$\frac{1}{2}$-$\frac{3}{4}$ tsp. powdered ginger

maraschino cherries — optional

What you do is, you use about 32 oz. of canned peach halves (or, probably better, fresh peaches that are peeled or whatever you do to peaches, pare them probably and pits removed. I've never actually tried this with *real* raw peaches, but it's got to be better now that I think about it. I'm just too lazy). Mash 'em up in a bowl. Add about 2 tablespoons of cornstarch to about $\frac{2}{3}$-$\frac{3}{4}$ of the syrup that came with the canned peaches, or else maybe 2 cups of water and 5 tablespoons sugar. This can turn out as sweet as you want it, depending if you're planning on it for a soup or dessert. Okay, the syrup goes in a pan with a tablespoon of melted shortening. I don't know why but when I see recipes for fruit soups they always do it, so I'll do it here, too. Mix the cornstarch-syrup-shortening up well. Add the mashed peaches, stirring constantly over a medium heat. Add about $\frac{1}{2}$-$\frac{2}{3}$ teaspoon powdered ginger, or less or more, if you like ginger. Bring the whole thing to a boil, and then simmer for a few minutes, stirring, stirring. Now, see, this is one of those basic recipes. You can ad lib like crazy, make ginger peachy soup cookies, maybe. You can serve the thing hot, or cold, for soup or dessert. If you want it loose, at the end you can mix in more of the syrup. I suppose you could add other things. (Who am I to say thee nay?) I think of adding maraschino cherries, for one. It just depends on your tolerance for this sort of thing. I think it would go great with my fabled pear pie.

HARLAN ELLISON

Café Ellison Diabolique

freshly-ground coffee (see note below)

El Popular Mexican-style brick chocolate

$1\frac{1}{2}$ tsp. C&H Hawaiian washed raw sugar (or equivalent brand)

$\frac{1}{4}$ tsp. nutmeg

$\frac{1}{4}$ tsp. cardamom

raw honey

whipping cream (not milk, not half-&-half)

12-ounce coffee mug

mortar and pestle

NOTE: Any good coffee will do. But by "any" I mean any whole bean or freshly-ground, not canned. Jamaican Blue Mountain, Kona, Celebes Kalossi, Guatemala Antigua, Honduras Estrieta, Sumatra Mandheling, as well as any medium-dark Brazilian will serve. Do not use flavored coffees — with chocolate or vanilla or macadamia or suchlike. But if you wish to duplicate the original, the recommended blend is as follows:

70% Mexican Coatepec

20% Colombian Supremo

10% French Roast

Into a 12-ounce coffee mug spoon the raw sugar, cardamom, nutmeg, and a drizzle (about $\frac{1}{2}$ a teaspoon) of raw honey (more or less, to taste).

With a mortar and pestle break off and pulverize sufficient El Popular Mexican chocolate from the brick cakes in the 15-ounce package to produce 2 full teaspoons of finely-crushed grind. Add it to the contents of the mug.

Get the coffee into the mug. Preferably a drip method, a Melitta filter or one of the European small pots that doesn't produce an acidic residue or oily film, as one gets with a percolator. Use boiling water. Leave about an eighth of the mug for the addition of cream, producing a golden hue. Stir like crazy.

This is my personal coffee recipe, refined over the past twenty-eight years to produce a cuppa that can be slogged away all day. For those who need their coffee dead-black and harsh, forget this. For those who truly like the taste of coffee but don't want heartburn or the jangles, who take cream and sugar . . . welcome home. This one produces a balance between the harsh, often unpleasant taste of regular coffee and the cloying sweetness of hot cocoa. While it bears lineal ties with Russian Coffee and Café Chocolat, the addition of nutmeg and honey give it a piquancy all its own. I find that a steaming mug prepared in this fashion early in the morning soothes the jangled stomach lining yet furnishes the push to get to work at whatever's in the typewriter from the night before. During the day, it can be sipped even when cold, almost like an iced dessert coffee. At night it is companionable, and not to be dismissed in its estimable service as a mild aphrodisiac. (Thus the adjective in its title.)

An earlier version of this recipe appeared in the 1973 edition of *Cooking Out of This World*, a wonderful Ballantine original that included Walter M. Miller, Jr.'s excellent recipe for Gopher Stew, the very same recipe I included with the dead gopher I mailed by 4th Class Mail to the comptroller of Signet Books when he wouldn't release the rights to one of my books. That story, like the recipe for coffee here proffered, has become legend.

This is the wonderful brew eighteen years later. It has undergone changes and refinements, but remains a particular favorite of the many guests at Ellison Wonderland. Ben Bova, Robert Silverberg, Norman Spinrad, Edward Bryant, and others beg like children when they come to visit. Susan thinks it's too sweet, but then she's a Brit who takes tea in the morning, with milk. This is why we won the Revolutionary War.

CAROL EMSHWILLER

I do have a couple of recipes that seem to be me or mostly mine. One problem: I make them "by ear" and the last two times I've put out hamburger to defrost for my meatloaf in order to find out what I really do when I make it, the kids overwhelmed me with three strong votes for spaghetti instead. Anyway, here it is, roughly. I'll try to try it out before I send this letter. (You can guess from these recipes that I am a wheat germ, brown rice, whole wheat, soybean kind of person, though NOT macrobiotic. I "believe in" meat. But I did learn the basic premises for the bread from a macrobiotic friend — who by the way, and if it's of any interest, is a young man in the Nickolais Dance Co. and carries a trunk full of macrobiotic foods and cooking utensils whenever he goes on tour so he can do all his own cooking wherever he is.)

Everything Meatloaf

1 lb. ground beef

2 eggs

$\frac{1}{2}$ of 8-oz. can Chinese water chestnuts, quartered

about $\frac{1}{2}$ cup sesame seeds

about $\frac{1}{4}$ cup sunflower seeds (not salted)

about $\frac{1}{4}$ cup coarsely chopped almonds

about $\frac{1}{4}$ cup wheat germ

1 chopped onion

1 small grated carrot

some chopped green pepper

(more)

79

salt and pepper

lemon juice, about 1 tbsp.

liquid — I guess about $\frac{1}{4}$ cup water, milk, or tomato juice

Mix it all up and cook like meatloaf — 350° F. for about 1 hour.

Anything Bread

1 cup whole wheat flour or mixture of other flours

3 eggs

$1\frac{1}{2}$ tsp. baking powder

$\frac{1}{4}$ to $\frac{1}{2}$ cup sunflower seeds

$\frac{1}{4}$ cup coconut

$\frac{1}{2}$ cup or more sesame seeds

$\frac{1}{4}$ to $\frac{1}{2}$ cup wheat germ

about 2 tbsp. oil

$\frac{1}{2}$ cup raisins

1 or 2 tbsp. honey or molasses

Enough liquid (milk or water) to moisten

How much liquid depends on how much of the other ingredients you've used. Just make it the usual consistency for quick breads. You may leave out or alter nuts and seeds to change flavors.

DAVID GERROLD

Serendipity Curry

I have to call this Serendipity Curry because it happened accidentally. It tastes awful, and takes much too long to prepare, but I find it's a great way to use up a lot of ingredients in a hurry. I start by taking a steak, or any meat that is probably too good for me, and cutting it into what dog-food manufacturers would call bite-sized chunks. Then I soak it in rum and sprinkle it with lemon-pepper. (I sprinkle everything with lemon-pepper.) While this is marinating (a couple of days or so), make some rice. I usually use MJB and follow the directions on the package for steaming, as boiling is supposed to drain valuable nutrients. (I make enough rice for four servings because I like leftovers.) While the rice is steaming, I put the meat chunks in a frying pan and grill them until they are edible — I guess this could be called cooking to taste. Then I put them aside and put the rice in a frying pan. (Or as much of it as will fit. The thing about cooking rice is that if you cook more than you need at any one time, it doesn't go to waste; you can use it all week long. So whenever I make rice, I always overcook. You'd be surprised how much rice you can use up this way.)

Anyway, into this frying pan of rice I add two or three eggs and proceed to scramble them — producing an odd combination called scrambled eggs and rice. With a half-teaspoon of sugar added, this can be an interesting breakfast. With a dollop of ketchup, it becomes the basis for this serendipitous curry. Add some curry powder or even a small (very small) can of prepared curry sauce. You have to figure out your own proportions on these things. Because this is one of those recipes that is made "to taste," there is no way to do it wrong. I suspect that there is also no way to do it right.

Add the meat now. Just pour it on top. Or stir it in. If you're adventurous, add some pineapple chunks too. By now, it should be edible. If it isn't, put it in a warm oven for a while and give everything a chance to settle. This is one of those recipes where some of the ingredients have to overcome their basic antagonism toward each other. Once I added some peach chunks — that didn't work. Another time I added some corn and green pepper and tomato slices. That was interesting too. If anyone comes up with any odder variations, I would appreciate not hearing about them.

MARC HAEFELE

Cosmic Minestrone

This elegant ordination of Vegetables hath found coincidence or imitation in sundry works of art.

— T. Browne

I don't believe in recipes. The only two things you can cook that need a recipe are soufflés and puff pastries. So here is a formulation for Cosmic Minestrone. Where I live, there is a great demand for it. Since the onset of tomato season this fall, I have made about 75 gallons, 3 gallons at a batch, and, I am certain, I have never made one batch taste like another. The variations are significant, because the making of soup ought to be a process of languorous experimentation. If it is, it will offer many homely fulfillments for nondescript little creative impulses you never knew you had. Indeed, the only possible way you could make soup-making a bore would be in following some recipe or another slavishly.

The best time of the year to make Cosmic Minestrone is during the tomato season, which happens from the end of September to the beginning of November where I live.

Ingredients:

With one exception, any one or two ingredients can be sub-stituted; most can, singly, be omitted. But if you leave out more than any one thing, you better replace it with something of your own devising: butter for cooking oil, for instance. The one ingredient you cannot substitute is time. For at least three hours, the soup must be uppermost in your mind. You may do anything else you like during much of this time, but you must not forget the kettle, and it shouldn't really be out of your sight.

Get a large pot: I use a number 10 (3-gal.) thick aluminum kettle. (I wish I had something bigger.) Soak the beans in advance, overnight.

$\frac{1}{2}$ to $1\frac{1}{2}$ lbs. of fresh onions, chopped

not more or not much more than one $\frac{1}{2}$-cup cooking oil

2-6 cloves garlic, chopped (to taste, right?)

spices (very flexible):

1 tbsp. oregano

1 tbsp. sweet basil

1 tbsp. cumin

2 bay leaves

1 tsp. marjoram

1 tsp. turmeric

1 tsp. thyme

pinches (ad lib.):

rosemary, tarragon, coriander, chili, sambar maybe, and a bit of chervil; plus something of your own

2-5 lbs. of tomatoes. (If tomatoes are out of season, you might as well use the Italian canned kind.)

1 or 2 lbs. of white and/or red beans

$\frac{1}{4}$ (or thereabouts) cups of dried sweet corn

$\frac{1}{2}$ cup (or thereabouts) of white or (of course preferably) brown or wild rice

(more)

84

a collection of *fresh vegetables*, which might include all or some of the following:

several carrots (if garden-fresh, chop and include greens), up to 5

1 or 2 (no more) turnips, small (a small turnip is one you can barely conceal in your hand; or a similar portion of a large turnip)

at least $\frac{1}{2}$ of a large bunch of celery, chopped; with leaves if possible

1 large fresh green or red pepper

1-2 small hot peppers

2 or 3 scallions, or the white part of a leek

a few beet greens

a couple of large potatoes, scrubbed but not peeled, chopped into a dozen pieces each

small quantities of spinach and/or parsley (more than 6 leaves of the one or a bunch of the other would be redundant) (but not harmful)

perhaps a handful of coarsely chopped green beans, or shelled fresh peas

1 cup of chopped fresh cabbage, or lettuce

seasonal wild vegetables, like wild garlic or sorrel, a chopped handful

maybe a can of anchovies

1 quart of water, more to be added as seems necessary

salt to taste, as you go, beginning latterly

If you, like me, are in the agreeable habit of guzzling beer or wine while cooking, the very least you can do is to offer the pot a healthy swig now and then.

[This soup is not one that can be cut down to lesser quantities successfully. Expect to arrive at three gallons minimum. — *This note elicited in conversation.* — ED.]

Method:

Take your big pot, and put the chopped onions and garlic and oil in it over a high flame. When they begin to sizzle, add the spices — bay leaves last. Stir until everything turns a nice yellow-brown. Add beans. Stir for two minutes. Add at least a quart of water, and reduce flame. When it begins to simmer, add anchovies if you want to add anchovies. Stir some more. Add those tomatoes, which if fresh will have been chopped in eighths unless they are plum-sized, with which quarters are okay. Stir until the soup starts simmering again, add corn and rice, then taste. See if you like what is going on. It will need salt — a fairly large amount, but don't get carried away. Add a little at a time, to taste. Or try soy sauce. Chop vegetables up to your favorite size; add in about the above order. Do not add them all at once. Just one vegetable at a time, and the whole process should take about a half hour. Or more. Simmer whole pot for another hour, stirring and tasting, tasting, tasting. Then put pot on lowest possible fire, have a last taste, and put a lid on the pot. Sit down and think if there is anything else you could put in to make it taste better. If there is, add some. Now, cook over that lowest flame for another hour, checking up on the soup as per the instructions above. The soup will then be ready to serve. I usually serve mine with a dollop of fresh-grated cheese or a big hunk of sour cream in each bowl, but I certainly can't say no one finds this a bit excessive.

Along with the soup, the favored tipple is either Rolling Rock Extra Pale premium beer, or a nice cheap red wine.

The soup will last indefinitely, or at least until all your friends find out about it.

JOE L. HENSLEY

Rocket Head Cheese Ball

1 jar Kraft Old English
  Cheese
1 jar Cheese & Bacon (or
  Ver-a-sharp)
1 small triangle
  Roquefort
1 8-oz. package
  Philadelphia Brand
  Cream Cheese

2 tsp. finely chopped
  onion
a pinch salt
$\frac{1}{2}$ package chopped
  pecans (4-oz. pkg.)

Combine and mix the cheeses. Blend in finely chopped onion, salt, and chopped pecans. Mix very well and refrigerate till firm. Shape into ball and roll ball in remainder of chopped pecans and a liberal sprinkling of parsley flakes. Spread on crackers or party rye.

Very therapeutic for hangovers — hence the name. Improves in taste if allowed to rest twenty-four hours in the refrigerator before eating.

FRANK HERBERT

Beef in Oyster Sauce

1 lb. tenderloin or sukiyaki beef sliced thin across grain

1 tsp. minced garlic

6 green onions, chunked

3 tbsp. soy sauce

$\frac{1}{3}$ cup oyster sauce (buy from Oriental grocery)

$\frac{1}{3}$ cup thinly sliced green pepper

1 tsp. sugar

$\frac{1}{4}$ cup saki (or good Chablis)

1 tsp. minced ginger (*fresh* ginger)

$\frac{1}{2}$ cup beef stock

$\frac{1}{2}$ cup Japanese mushrooms

cornstarch

Cut beef in small, thin slices. Butcher can do this for you on slicing machine, or you can freeze the meat and cut it while still partly frozen. Slice (thin) onions, mushrooms. Coat meat with cornstarch, mix with mushrooms. Mix beef stock, oyster sauce with 1 (one) tbsp. cornstarch. Heat 2 (two) tbsp. oil in bottom of a wok. Toss-cook garlic, green onions, and pepper until lightly translucent; remove from oil and keep warm. Cook meat and mushrooms in oil about one minute, tossing as it cooks. Add sugar, ginger, soy, and wine to stock mix; bring to boil separately.

Return garlic, green onions, and pepper to meat mixture, pour the hot sauce mix over the meat, etc. Serve immediately with steamed rice.

This will serve four normal human beings or two hungry science fiction types. Poul and Karen Anderson and Jack and Norma Vance once polished off three times this recipe measurement plus generous servings of Peking goose. Of course, Bev and I helped them somewhat.

Peking Goose

1 tender whole goose

$\frac{1}{2}$ cup honey

$1\frac{1}{2}$ tsp. salt

4 tbsp. red vegetable sauce (A canned sauce made from garlic, soy beans, and red rice, available from Chinese grocery; or make your own by milling in blender one part garlic to four parts soy beans to two parts red rice.)

$1\frac{1}{2}$ tsp. raw sugar (NOT the so-called "clean-raw." Get the true raw sugar, from health food store if necessary.)

1 cup boiling water

3 tbsp. Oriental rice wine or a good white (Chablis or sherry)

$1\frac{1}{2}$ tsp. five-fragrances spice (Absolutely essential; get it from a Chinese grocery.)

$1\frac{1}{2}$ tsp. white wine vinegar

Chinese plum sauce (plum butter makes an excellent substitute)

Clean the goose and check for pinfeathers, then submerge it in a large pot of boiling water for 2 (two) minutes. Drain and dry the skin with towel. Take an icepick and gently stab through the fat layer all over the skin — perforations about a quarter of an inch apart *all over it*. Pop in a preheated oven (450° F.) for 2 (two) minutes. Combine honey and cup of boiling water and place in shallow pan (large cookie pan is excellent). Roll the goose in the honey mixture, using hands to spread it; cover the entire skin. Hang goose to drain over the honey pan. After two hours, rub inside of goose with salt and five-fragrances spice mixture, then repeat immersion of goose in honey, covering entire skin. Repeat treatment with honey every two hours for about ten hours. Hang the goose for a total of 24 hours (including the ten hours of honey treatment). Hang it always by the neck. This is easier if you can get a goose with the head still attached. Skin should be hard to the touch when it has dried sufficiently. Mix the red vegetable sauce, vinegar, wine, and sugar and coat the inside of the goose generously. Roast over open barbecue and serve with small circles of unleavened white bread (the soft Oriental or Greek style) and Chinese plum sauce.

If you do not have a barbecue, you can use your regular oven with the following technique: Use a pan with a shallow amount of water in it; place the goose on a rack well out of the water. Preheat oven to 400° F. and roast goose for about 25 minutes or until it is lightly browned; reduce heat to 275° F. and roast 40 minutes to three hours longer depending on size of goose — about $\frac{1}{2}$ hour a pound at 275° F. — basting frequently with drippings. Turn oven off, but leave door closed; allow goose to remain in oven for another 20 to 30 minutes. You want a dark brown color and crackly skin.

Sukiyaki

Sukiyaki (pronounced skiyaki) is more a way of life than a recipe. Once you get the hang of it, you can play many variations on the theme. Insist on the freshest vegetables you can get. The meat must be sliced very thin. The technique of layering in a pan should follow the dictum: vegetables requiring most cooking go farthest down in the pan. Using this technique, you can actually cook sukiyaki very rapidly in quite a deep kettle, making certain that the top layer of meat covers all the greens and seals in the mixture.

The rule of thumb is $\frac{1}{4}$ to $\frac{1}{2}$ pound of beef per person. Remember that there is no single master sukiyaki recipe. It should be served with rice, and the best way to cook it is at the table in front of your guests. We often use an electric skillet. You can use a hibachi if you take off the grill and set the pan right into the coals, but prepare the pan first off the heat until you learn to layer the food into it rapidly.

Prepare your seasoning mixture ahead of time and have it ready at hand when you start to cook.

Seasoning mixture:

$\frac{3}{4}$ cup soy sauce (Japanese *shoyu* preferred)

$\frac{1}{2}$ cup raw sugar (real raw sugar, NOT the so-called "clean-raw")

3 tbsp. saki

1 cup hot water

1 tsp. minced fresh ginger

Cook your hot rice timed to serve when the sukiyaki is ready.

The Sukiyaki for four persons:

2 lbs. thinly sliced sukiyaki beef, cut across the grain (tenderloin preferred)

1 piece of beef kidney suet (about 2" x 3" by $\frac{1}{2}$")

1 large white onion sliced very thin

1 bunch of green onions cut in about 2-inch lengths

1 block of fresh bean cake (tofu) cut in 1-inch squares

1 cup of fresh bean sprouts

1 can (16 oz.) of bamboo shoots sliced thinly lengthwise

1 small package of bean thread softened ahead of time in hot water

$\frac{1}{2}$ pound fresh mushrooms sliced rather thickly lengthwise

1 pound of fresh spinach broken into bite-size pieces and pre-cooked about one minute in boiling water

Heat pan until suet sizzles. Swish suet around to coat entire inner surface of pan. Add meat and brown it lightly, then remove to side dish. Recoat pan with suet oil. Place layer of sliced onions in bottom, add layer of bamboo shoots, mushrooms, tofu, bean sprouts (I dry them first lightly in oven to remove some of the moisture), green onion; top with layer of spinach to cover entire contents right to edge of pan and do the same with the thinly sliced meat. I generally add the seasoning mixture at the tofu layer, using just enough of it to come up to the bottom of the tofu. At this time, you can open up a small circle in the center of the mix and introduce bean thread or *shirataki*. The sukiyaki is done when spinach is tender to probing with chopsticks: 5 to 8 minutes.

Vegetables we have added to our Sukiyaki with lipsmacking success:

Fresh tomatoes (skinned, sliced, and squeezed to remove excess water)

Asparagus (very fresh young shoots sliced once lengthwise)

Chinese cabbage (this tends to dominate unless you braise it first in suet oil and add as spinach layer)

Green pepper (treat lightly, as with Chinese cabbage)

Fresh corn (remove from cob and substitute for bean sprouts, placing in center cavity with bean thread)

Chinese snow peas (slice thinly lengthwise and place directly atop the white onions)

Summer squash (sliced *very* thin and placed atop bottom onion layer as substitute for bamboo shoots)

The most successful variations on the sukiyaki theme avoid a one-flavor domination.

Always leave the suet in the pan while cooking. It continues to give off oil which adds a marvelous flavor to the finished dish. It's normal for the pan to smoke a little at the start.

There are as many variations on how to cook sukiyaki (and the proper ingredients to use) as there are districts in Japan. Some prefer a very shallow pan, with meat cooked first about one minute, then pushed into corner of pan, vegetables added each in its own pocket of the pan, enough seasoning sauce added to just gently simmer the dish, green onions added last. Most recipes call for high heat all the way, however, and quick cooking to a slightly crisp *al dente* for vegetables. Some cooks prefer to omit the ginger; others add it as a few thin slices to the pan right after the suet coating. Some prefer more green onions and a sharp reduction in the sliced white onion. Some prefer no white onion at all.

If you're cooking it at the table, start your guests with a thin Japanese soup to enjoy while you're cooking. Generally, sukiyaki is served with a table setting of three bowls at each place: 1 for the sukiyaki, 1 for rice, and 1 for a raw egg (into which you dip each bite as you take it). A variation on this is to lightly poach the eggs in a bit of the seasoning mixture or in the pot broth, then serve one each for dipping in the yolk. Some poach the eggs right in the pan, opening a center cavity for it at the appropriate moment.

The rice is served and eaten plain to renew the palate between bites of the other food.

Serve small cups of hot saki with this dish and it becomes a pure delight.

The above is just an introduction to sukiyaki cookery. I urge you to experiment. Remember: *very* fresh vegetables. Get the cooking times correct (thin slicing helps with the ones which require longer cooking time). Supreme success is when all of the ingredients cooked in one pot come out "just right."

Go thou and do likewise.

H. H. HOLLIS

Guacamole

1 ripe avocado

1 ripe, ripe tomato

1 large lime or two small
  ones

1 small chili pepper or
  half a large one

$\frac{1}{2}$ small onion or 4-5
  green onions

salt and black pepper

If you are the kind who lets the grocer pick your produce, do not attempt a guacamole. The secret lies in selecting the avocado and there is not a grocer anywhere in the world who knows how to do this. "Here is two nice ones," they say with an engaging piratical smile, "just right for eating tonight." The two proffered will, indeed, be beautiful to the sight: sleek, green, polished like jade . . . and of the same internal consistency. Sam Houston never ate an alligator pear like that, and I do not propose to do so either.

The perfect avocado for the superb guacamole should yield to the touch. It should not spring back fully. When the whole fruit is enclosed in the hand and gently s-q-u-e-e-z-ed, gently! it should impart the sensation that a very little more pressure would cause the object to burst. Remember, we are going to eat it, not mail it. Now buy it and take it home.

Take a medium-sized white onion (in the scale: pearl, cocktail, little bitty, small, medium, large, very large). Cut it in half. Peel

95

the half you intend to use. Cut it in pieces, about a dozen. Put these in the bottom of the blender container, so they will be the first things attacked by the blades. If you don't have a white onion, use the white parts of four or five spring onions. (Yes, peel them and cut off the roots. ¿Cómo no?)

Cut the avocado in half, the long way. Dispose of the seed. It is only a *bubbameisseh* that leaving the seed in the mix will keep it from turning brown. What keeps guacamole from turning brown is the lime juice (and being eaten up very quickly). If the papery skin of the seed has clung to the fruit instead of to the seed, take a teaspoon and scrape it out, being careful not to take any flesh of the avocado. Cut the avocado in quarters and peel each quarter. If it is really ripe, the skin should come away very easily, and the outside of the fruit should be a very soft layer which is a rich Paris green in color. As you peel each quarter, dice it into the blender on top of the onion pieces. When the whole avocado has been cut up, salt and pepper the mix to taste (about $\frac{1}{2}$ to $\frac{3}{4}$ tsp. salt and $\frac{1}{4}$ to $\frac{1}{2}$ tsp. black pepper is my taste). Squeeze half a large lime or a whole small one over the mix, washing down the salt and pepper with the lime juice.

Quarter a tomato. Cut out the pulp and seeds into the blender, discarding the skin and rind. Salt and pepper the tomato properly and cut the pieces smaller, reaching into the blender with your knife to do so. Pick out a chili pepper about the size of May's thumb, or half the size of Hollis' [Editor's Note: H. H. Hollis has *long* fingers and big hands]. Cut off the pointed half (of the chili, not HHH's thumb). Put the other half back in the brine. Cut the part you are using into very small bits, on top of the tomato. (Yes, use the seeds. They add texture, taste, and a kick better than Serutan.) Squeeze the other half of a large lime, or another small lime, over all, cap the blender, and turn on for 3-4 seconds. Turn off. Uncap, reach in with your knife, and stir so that the next blending will bring the tomatoes and chili into the ambit of the blades. Blend for another 3-4 seconds, and so on until it is ready.

Remember! The object is not to puree the stuff. It is ready to eat when it is cohesive, but there should be chunks of avocado, bits of tomato, and just a few tiny shreds of chili still recognizable. This gives it texture, color, and the flavor of the real thing, and this is the reason that you cannot use frozen canned avocado paste. Indeed, if you have the patience, the whole production is better (and more Mexican) if you chop the onion very fine and mash the other ingredients in with a fork and a generous helping of elbow grease. However.

We serve guacamole as a dip, with tequila sours, Pimm's No. 1 Cup, or vermouth on the rocks. The recipe given is just a little too much for two people and not quite enough for four, so if you're having one couple over for dinner, it's just fine for the cocktail bit because it brings everybody to the table hungry. When we have any left over, we eat it for salad the next night. With a charcoaled steak, it is *¡Olé! ¡Olé!* All the way. And it can be served as the salad course of a regular dinner, provided the entree is also pretty strong flavored.

Huevos Rancheros

12 eggs

6 tortillas

$1\frac{1}{2}$ cups chopped onions

1 garlic clove, minced or pressed

butter enough (HHH calls it "schmaltz," i.e., chicken fat)

4 tomatoes, peeled and chopped

$\frac{3}{4}$ cup finely chopped sweet green peppers

1 small chili pepper or $\frac{1}{2}$ large one

$\frac{1}{2}$ tsp. salt

Huevos rancheros are not my idea of a breakfast dish. Too

97

long to prepare — and, like all the other hangover remedies in the pharmacopoeia of folklore, this one does not work, either. To put your guests on the road, still drunk but alert, they are unbeatable. That's the only time I ever cook huevos rancheros: late at night, and when everybody is looplegged. I have never had a complaint. Plenty of black coffee with them; and if there's a really compulsive drinker in the crowd, give him a cold beer with his and make him drink it from the bottle. The eggs, the tortillas, and the carbonation will fill him up and run him home.

Get a package or two of tortillas from the cold box at the supermarket. Warm them and keep them warm. Melt the chicken fat (or butter) in a saucepan. I use an enamelled iron one. Chop and mince the onion and the garlic clove: sauté five minutes. Chop up the vegetables, including the chili, and put into the saucepan with the hot fat, the onion, and the garlic. Salt and pepper to taste, remembering that the chicken fat already has some salt in it. Cover the whole and let simmer ten minutes.

Uncover and simmer the sauce ten more minutes. Fry two eggs sunnyside up or over easy for each person (in butter for me, please), put the eggs on a tortilla in a plate (where else?), and spoon salsa *quan. suff.* over the eggs.

Like waffles: each celebrant should eat his as soon as he gets it. Lukewarm tortillas are tough. I don't know what to do with leftover sauce. I never have any.

Mancha Manteles

1 lb. lean pork, cut into small cubes	seasoned flour
3 lbs. chicken breasts and thighs, boned	2 tbsp. butter
	2 tbsp. olive oil

Sauce:

1 tbsp. blanched almonds

1 small can tomato sauce

1 tsp. sesame seeds

1 qt. boiling water

1 medium onion, chopped

1 tbsp. chili powder

1 medium green pepper, chopped

$\frac{1}{4}$ cup sugar

$\frac{1}{2}$ tsp. cinnamon

3 whole cloves

$\frac{1}{2}$ cup apples, peeled and cubed

1 bay leaf

1 medium sweet potato, cut in good-sized cubes

salt to taste

bananas

1 cup pineapple tidbits

We first had this at "a little restaurant around the corner" from the Hotel Geneve in Mexico City. We were taken there by a friend, and we had . . . never mind what else we had . . . it was all good . . . but *mancha manteles* is one of those magnificent natural dishes that have everything: aroma, color, texture, flavor, and aftertaste. It is rich, exotic, and easy to prepare. It makes the water come in my mouth just to think about it.

Start with the pork. It must be lean. Pour the olive oil (it must be olive oil) in a skillet. Put the butter in with it. It must be butter. Melt the butter and brown the pork in this mixture. Take the pork out when it is browned and put it in a large saucepan. May uses that enamelled cast iron or Mexican clay.

In the same skillet and the same fat, brown the chicken after dredging it in the seasoned flour. Remove the chicken from the skillet and put it in the saucepan with the pork. (It must be pork. We tried veal, and it's just not the same.) Put the almonds and sesame seed in the skillet in the same fat, fry a little, then add the onion and green pepper, and fry a while longer. The vegetables ought to pick up the crust in the pan. They do in our skillet.

Add the tomato sauce to this and put the whole mixture in the blender. Blend pretty well. Then mix with water, chili powder, sugar, cinnamon, cloves, bay leaf, and salt. Cook this for 10-15 minutes to marry the flavors, and put it through a sieve. Pour the sieved sauce over the pork and the chicken in the saucepan and simmer it for half an hour.

Throw in the sweet potatoes and let simmer another quarter hour. Next add the apple and pineapple, and simmer another few minutes.

We serve it in big soup plates and we slice the bananas right into it. Each bite is a new sensation. The name means "tablecloth stainer" . . . and it will, too; so we tie bibs on everybody.

VIRGINIA KIDD

Imam *(Ee-mom)*

Mme. Essipoff says this dish was originally named "The Imam Fainted with Delight When He Tasted of This." When it was placed before a certain science fiction author, and he was informed of its full name, he tasted and remarked: "James Blish is made of sterner stuff."

1 or more eggplant

tomatoes, canned or (dead-ripe) fresh

stewing lamb (with as much fat trimmed off as possible)

garlic — to taste: a little or a full clove or more, up to a small bulb entire

onions, coarsely chopped

Imam has no fixed quantities, and no certain outcome. Use as much as you think you would like of all of the ingredients. The onion and garlic are primarily for flavor (unless you are an onion freak, in which case use lots) and — roughly — the two vegetables and the lamb should be in equal proportions. Layer the ingredients in a largish casserole, and bake. Ultimately, according to the passer-on to me of this recipe, one arrives at a desired pudding-like consistency, where everything has cooked down into everything else and the flavors are well married. I prefer it when they are just sharing the same bowl but still individuals and recognizable as such. But if you want to serve it *very* soon after putting it in the oven, best to use leftover, already cooked cubed lamb. On the other hand, it can cook (at a low heat, 275°-300° F.) all day, or all afternoon. Fresh and preferably hot French or Italian bread should be served along with.

Marion's Spiced Coffee

Spiced coffee (cinnamon, clove, and a trace of ginger added just before serving and allowed to steep 2-3 minutes in the pot) might follow *Imam* or anything else that makes you feel vaguely Eastern.

Rawl Meat and Mushrooms

The following sauce is named for R.A.W. Lowndes. I checked it out with him for authenticity, and he replied:

"Tempting as the chance for immortality may be, I shall have to disown *Rawl Meat & Mushrooms*. I never made that concoction; what I did make was not in any sense of the word an 'emergency spaghetti sauce' — it was evolved because I was tired of having spaghetti always taste like tomato. My *Futurian Spaghetti* was, of course, similar in a number of ways, and wonderfully inexpensive in the early '40s; I could make a meal for three at 50¢ cost — which included, in addition to the above, a bag of delicious one-day-old pastry from the local bakery for a nickel."

His un-red spaghetti sauce has no cream of chicken soup in the ingredients but does add a can of kernel corn. Strange, this quite different dish is the way *I* remember it. Good either way.

1 tbsp. butter (or fat rendered from beef)

1 good-sized onion, coarsely chopped

1 good sized green pepper, coarsely chopped

1 lb. button mushrooms, tops only

$1\frac{1}{2}$ lbs. ground beef (not too fat)

1 can cream of chicken soup, condensed

1 can cream of mushroom soup, condensed

Sauté the onions and pepper in a small amount of butter or in some of the fat rendered while browning the ground beef; having sautéed them until just limp, set them aside. Brown the ground beef, disposing of excess fat. No seasonings are necessary, but you can experiment with a pinch of curry or the like, if you are so inclined. (However, this sauce is so quickly prepared that such herbs as thyme or oregano do not cook down properly — and the further away from traditional tomato-sauce seasoning you stay, the more un-usual it tastes.) Dump the contents of both cans of soup, *undiluted*, over the meat, stir until the mixture is warmed through, add the sautéed vegetables, and stir again. No further cooking is necessary. Meanwhile, sauté the mushrooms as little as possible — until done, to your taste. To cut down on skillet-washing, sauté mushrooms in advance, in the same pan, and set aside. Add mushrooms. When all is heated through, ladle onto spaghettini or a slice of home-baked bread. Garnish with fresh parsley. Serves 4 or more. (Canned mushrooms can be substituted, but it's not as pretty.)

URSULA K. LE GUIN

Crab Nebula

My friend Kay Michelfeld served us this one night, and I felt that both by its name and its nature it should be in this cookbook. Kay does not write recipes down, so the following is my interpretation of a ten minute phone conversation, and the truth is, neither of us *really* has the faintest idea how much crab she put in. But I know 3 goodsized Dungeness crabs will feed six people. Take it from there . . .

2 tbsp. butter

2 tbsp. flour

1 cup milk

$1\frac{1}{2}$ cups grated Tillamook cheese (or other American Cheddar)

2 cups Pacific crab (or Atlantic, or even lobster, but *not* King crab)

sherry, salt, pepper, parsley to taste

Make a cream-sauce with 2 tbsp. butter, 2 tbsp. flour, 1 cup milk. Add about $1\frac{1}{2}$ cup grated Tillamook cheese (or more — or less. Kay says that if you are unable to obtain Tillamook, you may use any inferior American Cheddar, but the difference will be noticeable unless you have a calloused palate.)

Now add about $\frac{1}{2}$ lb? 2 cups? — Well, add enough crab. (If you are unable to obtain Pacific crab, you may use those flabby little Atlantic ones, or even lobster; but if you are reduced to King

Crab, forget it.)

Flavor with sherry to taste, salt, pepper, parsley.

Serve on rice, or wild rice if you are J. Paul Getty, or English muffins, or whatever.

Fresh Gichymichy
(or to be honest about it, Nituke)

yam or sweet potato

carrots

mushrooms

Chinese cabbage or
    bok-choy

daikon radish or red
    radish

a leaf vegetable

burdock root (if possible)

2 tbsp. good soy sauce

garlic

squash of any kind
    (summer or winter)

cauliflower

broccoli

endive

celery

cabbage or kale

onion

1 tbsp. toasted sesame
    seeds, optional

You can use practically any vegetable you have around, and it doesn't have to be born yesterday, either; limp old green onions do just fine. The idea is to combine several, from a chaste and subtle combination of a few (Japanese style) to a crude hodge-podge of everything in the fridge (Gethenian style). It really doesn't matter, since each vegetable keeps its own particular flavor, cooked this way. I mean, it doesn't matter *much*.

I like to include yam or sweet potato, mushrooms, carrot, Chinese cabbage or bok-choy, daikon radish or red radish, and a leaf vegetable. Squash of any kind, summer or winter, is excellent, as well as cauliflower, broccoli, endive, celery, cabbage or

kale, burdock root if you can get it, onion. Garlic affects everything else, changing the nature of the dish somewhat.

Cut all the vegetables into *little matchsticks*. This sounds
revolting but it takes about 20 minutes, because (assuming you're
serving 4) the quantity of each vegetable is very small — one
small yam, for instance, one or two little zucchini, a carrot, 6 or
8 mushrooms, etc. So it goes very fast.

Heat a couple of tbsp. safflower or peanut oil very hot in frying
pan (if you have cut up the vegetables ahead of time and kept
them in water, be sure to drain them well or there will be a lot of
spitting). Cook the vegetables between 5 and 10 minutes, stirring
and watching constantly; 7 or 8 minutes should do it; they should
be semi-crisp and keep their color. Just before they're done add
a couple tbsp. good soy sauce, and 1 tbsp. toasted sesame seeds
if you like.

Serve with hot rice either as a main dish or a side dish.

Primitive Chocolate Mousse
(Also known as Mousse au chocolat,
Chocolate Moose, Brown Mouse, and
Please Sir I want some More.)

Included because it is curiously hard to find a good plain
responsible recipe for this extremely simple and impressive dish.
Serves 4:

2 oz. bitter chocolate	1 or 2 tsp. vanilla, brandy, rum, or bourbon
2 tbsp. water	
$\frac{1}{3}$ cup sugar	
4 egg whites, beaten stiff	$\frac{1}{3}$ pint whipping cream, whipped
4 egg yolks, well beaten	

Melt chocolate, water, and sugar in double boiler. If you can stir fast, forget the double boiler.

Beat egg whites stiff. Beat egg yolks well and add vanilla and liquor. Beat in chocolate mixture (cooled a bit); fold in the egg whites.

At this point the French often stop, but about $\frac{1}{3}$ pint whipping cream whipped can also be folded in, making it richer.

Chill at least 4 hours in individual dishes. You can make it the day before, in which case it gets spongy, which is equally pleasant.

FRITZ LEIBER

Fish Stew in Its Infinite Varieties

In a little hot olive oil, sauté to golden a sliced garlic bud, a big sliced onion, shreds of carrot and green pepper, sliced mushrooms, and any other vegetables that need this sort of softening. Takes maybe 20 minutes.

Meanwhile get every last bone out of any fish available, fresh or frozen — say halibut or red snapper or sole — and cut into chunks bite-size or a bit larger.

Add to golden-brown vegetables a cup or two of fish stock or of liquid from canned clams or any canned seafood not too outrageously salty, or of water. Stir. A couple of bay leaves go in nicely here. And some thyme or other herbs you fancy.

When this simmers, add your fish chunks, cover, and simmer 20 more minutes. Five minutes from finish add chunked tomatoes.

Add a teaspoon of lemon juice and a cup of white wine. Don't ever thicken with flour or the like. Season with salt and pepper, or do that earlier, like I do. Serve in bowls over toast if you want to, but not over rice. You're supposed to have achieved a broth filled with marine and vegetable goodies. My people love it, no kidding. And you've got yourself a meal that's low-starch, low-fat, low-calorie, but rich in protein, vitamins, and minerals. Also as cheap as you can make a good, hearty meal these days. Remember to use as little olive oil (or peanut oil or vegetable oil or even butter or margarine) as you can and still get the hard vegetables golden-brown.

Some Americans and even more American restaurants have the *idée fixe* that all fish should be deep fried, preferably in batter. You know — good old fish-and-chips and such. The Mediterranean French and Spaniards and the New Orleans folk know differently. Fish stew should be as regular an item of diet as stewed beef or chicken.

About the Infinite Varieties? Well, toward the end of simmering, just long enough to heat them up, add canned or fresh-boiled clams and shrimps. Good, but more expensive.

If you want to get really fancy, make the shrimp big — prawns — and add chunks of lobster and crab and strips of pimento. Then you've got a glamorous bouillabaisse, still more expensive, but very, very good. Of course there are pontificating, scholarly chefs, literati of the kitchen, who insist you can't make a true bouillabaisse without a sort of scorpion fish, *racasse* I think they call it, indigenous to Marseilles waters and now about fished to extinction. Myself, I eat such high-falutin', hair-splitting experts, toasted, for breakfast.

A final word on varieties of this fish stew, or unthickened chowder. You can vary the seasoning endlessly. Here I like curry best, just enough to kill the fish taste.

Some sea "foods" that you can't use are the dolphin or porpoise (which some Hawaiians eat as *mahi-mahi*), the sea lion, and whale. They're our intelligent fellow-inhabitants of Terra, and death and destruction to those who would cajole them to attack enemy frogmen or to plant underwater explosives!

MURRAY LEINSTER
(Will F. Jenkins)

Clams Casino, Frozen Oysters, and an Appetizer

I live in a house on the York River, which is an estuary of Chesapeake Bay. Since I have riparian rights, there are automatically oysters, clams, butterfish, and other seafood usually in my freezer. My latest favorite seafood is "Clams Casino." I don't know how widely known it is, but a good many people find it surprising:

First, of course, you catch your clams. Small to medium do very well. You open them to half-shells and put them in a baking dish. Then you use garlic salt (it may be used alone) or garlic and salt and pepper. To taste, of course. You add oregano and dredge bread-crumbs over the clams. You add a small square of bacon to the covering of each one, squeeze a dash of lemon-juice, and either bake or broil, again to taste, but you keep it up until the bacon is crisp. It is a superior comestible.

There's another much simpler thing to do with oysters, but it isn't a cookery recipe. I'd had a bushel or so of oysters hauled up on the beach for a picnic. There was an unusually cold night. I found some of the oysters frozen and partly opened. I tasted them. Oysters taste best when they're cold. Frozen oysters are as cold as you'll get. Some people don't like raw oysters because they're slimy. Frozen oysters have the texture of finely crushed ice.

This may sound absurd, but honestly that picnic was a party! They can be frozen in the freezing-chamber of your icebox, and frozen oysters are really something!

I hope this is the sort of thing you want: Did you ever spread buttered toast with raw ground lean meat and put Camembert on top for an antipasto? The Camembert is at least as good as the more usual caviar.

ROGER LOVIN

Lamb and Onion Burgundy

I got this one from an ancient American wino, who claims to have seen it in a vision, spread across the skies in letters of fire.

1 leg or shoulder roast of lamb (3 to 5 lbs.)	1 liter good burgundy wine
4 medium potatoes	wine or apple vinegar
4 medium sweet onions	spices as below
6 large carrots	

Heat a large, heavy pot and rub it with lard. Roll the roast in flour with salt, pepper, and $\frac{1}{4}$ cup sugar added.

Brown the roast on all sides (five minutes per side). Slice one onion and add while the roast is browning.

Clean all vegetables and quarter them. Add vegetables and $\frac{1}{4}$ liter wine to the pot. Cover, lower heat, and simmer 30 minutes. Add generous dash of vinegar, the rest of the wine, and a dash each of: tarragon, thyme, sassafras (optional), hot sauce, and paprika.

Cook another hour. Serve with sour bread, wine, and garnishes of bay leaves, lemon, or caraway seeds.

Tripe Delight Fantastic

This one I learned from an ancient Chinese vegetarian, to whom I had come for wisdom and cut-rate lessons in the more intricate forms of the pavane. Should be prepared while nude.

1 lb. honeycomb tripe	1 onion (med.)
1 lb. cherry tomatoes	$\frac{1}{4}$ cup finely chopped
$\frac{1}{2}$ lb. strip bacon	celery
1 lemon	spices as below

Cover tripe with cold water and bring to a boil. Drain and re-cover with salted water. Boil for one hour. After first half hour, add $\frac{1}{4}$ cup finely chopped onion and $\frac{1}{4}$ cup finely chopped celery.

Remove tripe and save liquid. Cut tripe into strips and roll in cracker dust. Place in boiler with bacon strips and whole cherry tomatoes. Broil on both sides, or until bacon is crisp.

Remove, add liquid, the rest of the onion (sliced), salt and pepper, and the lemon (sliced) . Place in broiler again for five minutes, then serve.

ROBERT A. W. LOWNDES

Here are a batch of my concoctions, as well as I can describe them. Procedures and some ingredients are variable, and the amount of almost anything I leave to inspiration. These recipes are general suggestions, and should be tried only by persons with instinct for cooking and an absence of conviction from hearsay, folklore, etc., about what is not edible or what is never done or what doesn't go with which. Such persons are to be pitied, although they may never die of indigestion. Actually, I have only one record of sickness from my efforts and that was myself when I undercooked the spaghetti once.

Brutally Whipped Potatoes

small potatoes with thin skins (red ones if you can find them)

shelled walnuts, as much as seems proper for the amount of potatoes (If either of your parents was a termite, then by all means crush the shells and include them.)

$\frac{1}{4}$ lb. of butter or margarine

up to $\frac{1}{2}$ lb. of sliced processed cheese

a splash of milk

optional: a sprinkle of Italian flavored bread crumbs

This calls for a large mixing pan or bowl and a hand electric mixer. Anathema and fallen armpits upon whomsoever shall peel the potatoes at any part of the process. While potatoes are boiling, place the butter or margarine at the bottom of the pan (if you can keep it at the top, you have a subject for profitable photography) and tear up and add as much sliced cheese as seems proper; then tear up a few slices more, adding them. Add the sprinkle of Italian bread crumbs and the walnuts (with or without shells, according to caution above) and the milk. Drain the potatoes when done, dump them in, and then go to it with the electric mixer — but ruthlessly, until all is homogenized except for the walnuts, and don't fret if they are, too. Either yellow or orange processed cheese will do; I can't tell much difference in flavor, but the orange produces a prettier end-product.

This recipe is not for Buddhists or anyone else who shrinks from torturing harmless vegetables.

Cosmic-Minded Sliced Beef Sandwich

2 large-size bread slices	hard crackers
beef	milk chocolate
tomato	sliced cheese
lettuce	mustard
mayonnaise	sliced onion

Few people have cosmic minds. Only one who has observed me make this sandwich has opined that perhaps it might be good, but he never tried it to see; one other drew the line at the hard crackers. Alas, the world is full of people who know something can't be good even though they've seen someone else thrive on it.

The cosmos is infinitely varied. I offer my suggestions as to the exact ingredients, but these not only can but should be varied according to individual preferences and availability. The order in which the sandwich is built is somewhat more important.

If you can find a large-sized type of rye bread called Kummisbrot, this is most desirable; next I would recommend a dark or light pumpernickel. However, as long as the bread is large size and not overly stale, it will work.

On one slice, smear mayonnaise, then add lettuce, tomato, and sliced beef. While I am partial to rare beef, nothing is wrong with medium or well done beef, so long as the texture is reasonably firm. Smear the other slice of bread with mustard, then place the sliced cheese and onion, and more sliced beef atop that. I prefer to alternate between Muenster and Swiss cheese, but this is optional; any cheese that slices rather than spreads will go well.

Place one layer of hard-type crackers — my preference is for Ritz, but you may have other favorites (the sort you might use for a dip will work very well) — upon each layer of sliced beef.

Now comes the center, which is a layer of milk chocolate, light if you use well done beef, dark if the beef is reddish or rare. (The less done the beef, the more likely it is to have a touch of sweetness of its own, so stronger chocolate will be wanted.)

Squooge the two sides of the sandwich lovingly together (not brutally so as to crush the tomato — which, I hope, is good and red, not pale pink), carve into sections if you like, and see if you can resist making another cosmic-minded sandwich when you've finished this one. If you can, you've either gone astray somewhere, are lacking in the cosmic mind, or are filled with anxiety over gaining weight. I can offer no hope for the last two afflictions.

Meatloaf Tortuga

The amount of various ingredients depends upon how large a meatloaf you want to make. If you want a small one, and have a freezer, why not make a large one, divide it in two, and put the second one away? It'll keep until you're ready.

chopped meat, whatever grade you prefer

light Puerto Rican rum

wheat germ

2 eggs

1 good-size onion, coarsely chopped

1 green or red sweet pepper, treated similarly

oatmeal

barbecue sauce, or catsup, hickory flavored (plain is acceptable if you can't get the flavored)

a splash of milk

minced garlic

optional:

Italian seasoning or other spices

Marinate the chopped meat overnight in a shot of rum. Suggest that you use no more the first time; if you find you might like a stronger piratical flavor, then use more rum the next time. The minimum will be effective, however. Fry onions and pepper in olive oil until golden. Spread out chopped meat at bottom of large mixing bowl and cover with a layer of minced garlic, then a layer of wheat germ. (Actually, since you'll have to end up squooging all this together by hand, it hardly matters about the order.) Add the eggs, oatmeal, milk, and contents of frying pan, transferred with a slotted spoon. (You do not, of course, want all the olive oil, but so much as gets through thus will be valuable to overall flavor.) Also include a noticeable dash of catsup. Make into loaf or loaves, then place those you're going to cook into refrigerator to cool for a few hours. Bake long at low temperature. A glaze of catsup on the top is optional, but splendid if you like catsup glaze.

If you change your mind and make the amalgamation into

hamburgers, pleasure will be extended over a longer period (assuming you have a freezer), and then you have *Hamburgers Tortuga*.

Veal Scallopine

1 huge onion, or 2 medium-sized ones, coarsely chopped

4 green or red sweet peppers (or 2 and 2 of each), likewise

2 small cans of tomato paste (preferably Italian)

up to a pound of mushrooms

2 lbs. of veal cutlet or veal cube steak (the latter is less costly and just about as good)

Madeira wine (optional, suggested by James Blish)

If you use wine, there are two possibilities: marinate the veal overnight in it, or add a shot or so to the liquid while it's bubbling. There is no need to waste the core and seeds of the peppers; they amalgamate very well. Fry the onions in olive oil until golden brown, then add the peppers, mushrooms, and veal in that order; veal to be cut into thin strips. Transfer the mass to a large pan (large enough for a pot roast — you'll need the space), then cover the top of the ingredients with (1) a layer of garlic powder, (2) a sprinkle of Italian seasoning. (If you do not have amalgamated Italian seasoning, then a touch of oregano, thyme, etc., will do, and a suggestion of ground clove is helpful.) Stir in the two cans of tomato paste. (Add water only if there does not seem to be sufficient liquid; contents of frying pan are NOT to be drained.) Bring concoction to a boil, then let it simmer, checking each half-hour or so to see if more liquid is needed. When meat is thoroughly done, turn off heat, cover, and let it stand until you're ready to devour it; then reheat. Serve on a base of egg noodles, spaghetti, or rice as you prefer, but noodles — the wide variety — are best. If your guests do not make pigs of themselves, you may have erred somewhere; however, they may just be insensitive. In any event, it's even better the next day, so don't worry about making too much.

I might add that if you cannot get veal cube steak (and cutlet is gruesomely expensive) several large veal chops mixed with chicken breasts do very well. Just more of a bother to cut up, but I was reduced to this measure the last time I made scallopine. It also goes very well with ham instead of the above two meats, and can even be made with beef, but I find it least tasty in that form.

WALLACE MacFARLANE
On Reading and Eating

. . . a few words about reading and eating. Or evaluate various foods against this standard. Sandwiches are dandy, but not loose floppy ones like chopped olive and cheese or many of the torpedoes. It is possible to distinguish one-hand and two-hand sandwiches and this is of consequence when reading a paperback. A stiff raisin pie may be eaten by hand, but gooey cherry is dangerous. Things like crackers and cheese and English onions and beer are great, of course. Soup is possible, but lumpy soup gets trickier. Spaghetti is ridiculous with a book. [Bananas, up to a certain degree of ripeness, are just fine for reading while snacking and vice versa — but not if you borrowed the book. Accidents *do* happen and a well bananaed book is useless for either reading *or* snacking. — ASST. ED.]

Another aspect is books to eat what by. If you are reading Mr. Lovecraft's decaying prose, Roquefort is not the thing to be nibbling. Grape juice may be uncomfortably close to the ichor of some BEM. A flan may be uncomfortable as well if a careless mad scientist is breeding bacteria in a culture medium.

ANNE McCAFFREY

Beignets

1 cup water
$\frac{1}{4}$ cup butter
$\frac{1}{4}$ cup finely chopped
   onion

1 cup flour
4 eggs

While this is the basic (without onions) mixture for cream puffs, these make a heavenly hot appetizer, or after-pub snack.

Boil the water in a saucepan with the butter. Immediately after the butter has melted, dump in the flour and beat madly until the dough "cleans the pot." Remove instantly from the heat. Add four eggs, one after another, beating until each has been incorporated in the batter. Add chopped onion.

Drop into hot fat by the teaspoonful and fry until brown — it doesn't take long. Then serve instantly to hungry guests. The above recipe makes enough for two dozen beignets.

Butterscotch Brownies

This is a quickie which my children, and unexpected guests, enjoy.

$\frac{1}{2}$ cup butter

$\frac{2}{3}$ cup brown sugar,
    tamped into cup

1 cup flour

1 egg

1 tsp. vanilla

$\frac{1}{2}$ cup nuts (except
    peanuts)

In a saucepan melt the butter and add the brown sugar until one has absorbed the other. Remove from heat and beat in the egg (quickly or the white fries). Add the flour, vanilla, and nuts and beat until blended. Turn into buttered 7" tin and bake in 350° F. oven for $\frac{1}{2}$ to $\frac{3}{4}$ hour. Can be undercooked and be chewy.

Carrots Kissimmee

1 lb. carrots, sliced
    cater-cornered

$\frac{1}{2}$ small onion, minced

$\frac{1}{2}$ orange finely chopped,
    peel and all

salt

tsp. sugar

3 tbsp. butter

The newer the carrots the better, but this treatment will muchly improve the flavor of any old carrot you happen upon in the refrigerator.

Combine carrots, onion, orange, salt, and sugar in a saucepan and add just enough water so that the carrots are *not* covered by the water level. Cook covered until carrots are tender, preferably until most of the liquid is reabsorbed. Add butter and serve.

Irish Clear Lamb Stew

Some dishes, in memory, are enhanced beyond the possibility of duplication. One of these *was* clear Irish lamb stew. I say *was* because the quality of the ingredients affected the final product. These are once again available to me in the Emerald Isle.

3 lbs. stew lamb
  (shoulder preferably,
  or neck and ribs with
  sufficient meat left on
  the bones)
salt and freshly ground
  black pepper

1 package frozen peas
$\frac{1}{4}$ to $\frac{1}{2}$ cup chopped fresh
  parsley, if possible
5 medium-large potatoes,
  peeled and cubed

You can stew a complete shoulder in one piece with the bones. Place meat in large pot (pressure cooker if you have one) and cover with water. Add some salt and several large grinds of fresh pepper. Cook the hell out of the meat until it is ready to fall off the bones. (I've used low pressure for one hour to achieve this end, or at least three hours of ordinary simmering.)

Remove the meat from the pot, reserving the broth. Remove meat from the bones in small, bite-size pieces. At this stage it comes away from the bones in layers and can easily be de-fatted and cut into small portions. (As we have a cholesterol problem, I am assiduous in removing the animal fat from the meat. *Chacun à son gout.*) I also skim a good bit of the excess fat from the broth, though a good deal is reabsorbed into the potato.

Half an hour before serving, add the potatoes and parsley and check the seasoning. Five minutes before serving, add the frozen peas; allow them to heat thoroughly. Serve in bowls with fresh biscuits or bread. Serves 4-6.

Irish (?) Potato Pancakes

My grandmother used to make these from leftover mashed (creamed) potatoes and my brothers and I would snarl and fight to get the first off the skillet and consume the most.

2 cups (or more) cold mashed potato

1-2$\frac{1}{2}$ cups flour

dollops of butter

Knead flour into the cold mashed potato on a floured surface. The quantity of flour required to make the rollable dough differs with the quantity of potato used and its texture, but you should have a cohesive mass much like bread dough and about the same consistency.

Roll this dough onto a floured board until $\frac{1}{4}$" thick. Cut into servable portions and fry on buttered skillet until golden brown on both sides. *My* children like syrup, honey, or jelly/jam with the pancakes, which I consider rank heresy. Plain butter and lots of it is sufficient.

Fried Rice

1 cup or more leftover cold rice

6-8 rashers bacon, finely chopped before cooking

2 eggs

2 tbsp. soy sauce

any leftover vegetables, green pepper, onion, meat available

Like most Chinese dishes, the trick to this one is to avoid overcooking, to allow the individual textures of the ingredients to retain their character.

Fry the bacon bits until brown and remove to absorbent towel. Sauté onion (green pepper, mushrooms, if available) until transparent. Sauté quickly any leftover meat, chicken, fish until warmed. Remove from pan.

Add enough cooking oil to make three tbsp. fat in pan. Brown rice quickly, stirring frequently. When rice appears warm, add soy sauce. I say 2 tbsp. but you may need more depending on the quantity of rice used. Rice should be light brown.

Stir in bacon, onion (et cetera), and meat and warm thoroughly with rice.

Then, pushing this mixture to side of pan, rapidly scramble two beaten eggs. As soon as they are cooked, fold in rest of ingredients and serve immediately. Tasty and filling.

Cold Apple Soup

4 cups of chopped tart
  peeled apples

3 cups dry red wine

grated rind of a lemon

1 tbsp. melted currant
  jelly

$\frac{1}{2}$ cup of sugar

juice of the lemon

1 tbsp. cinnamon

dash of salt

Simmer and puree the apples, sugar, and spices. Add the wine, juice of the lemon, and melted currant jelly. Cover, chill and serve.

Elsie Lee's Carrot Soup

This recipe I conned out of my favorite gothic author, Elsie Lee, who is a fabulous cook. I use this underhanded method of getting a fine recipe into this volume.

9 scraped, sliced carrots	3 cups chicken stock
3 stalks sliced celery	2 tbsp. minced parsley
1 sliced onion	a few drops Tabasco
1 bay leaf	$\frac{1}{2}$ cup heavy cream
2 cloves	

Cook over moderate heat until the vegetables are very tender. Work through a sieve and add two tbsp. minced parsley and a few drops of Tabasco. Chill thoroughly. Stir in $\frac{1}{2}$ cup heavy cream at serving time and add croutons.

(Tip: sauté the vegetables first in a bit of butter. Then puree and add to chicken stock.)

Tuna Delight

I can't imagine a mother with a growing family who hasn't used this universal favorite . . . but then, this cookbook may go out of *this* world — and universe.

1-2 cans tuna fish (or salmon)	1 can condensed mushroom soup
1 10-oz. package potato chips ("crisps" to Europeans)	$\frac{1}{2}$ chopped onion (optional)
	$\frac{1}{2}$ tbsp. chopped parsley (optional)

Drain tuna fish/salmon. Mash the potato chips/crisps until small. Dump in tuna fish/salmon and condensed soup, onion, and parsley. Mix ingredients thoroughly. Turn into greased 2-qt. casserole. Pop into 350° F. oven for $\frac{1}{2}$ to $\frac{3}{4}$ hour or until bubbling and crisp. I like the crust myself. Serve with salad for 4-6.

Any leftovers make a good spread for cocktail time the next night — if there are any leftovers.

Veal Tarragon

This got served frequently at Milford because it was easy for me to prepare in the rather sparsely supplied cottage at Myers' when I a-Milfording went and cooked for the bachelors there.

1 good-sized veal cutlet, Italian or regular, per person

1 can condensed mushroom or celery soup

$\frac{1}{2}$ cup dry white wine or vermouth

$\frac{1}{2}$ tsp. tarragon, fresh if at all possible

salt and pepper to taste

Brown veal in heavy skillet. Remove. Add condensed soup to pan and allow it to absorb the meat juices and crust. Add the wine and tarragon, and stir to combine. Replace meat, simmer covered for $\frac{1}{2}$ hour. Serve with rice and salad. For dessert use Ursula K. Le Guin's *Chocolate Mousse.*

Zucchini Zuperb

1 lb. zucchini

1 medium-sized onion,
    finely chopped

salt and pepper to taste

1 tsp. sugar

plenty of butter

Wash and chop zucchini. I run the knife down the center to quarter it and then slice off $\frac{1}{4}$-inch rounds right into the pan.

Add chopped onion, sugar, salt and pepper, and $\frac{1}{2}$ cup water.

Cook covered tightly. When tender, add the butter. This dish does not get ruined if guests are enjoying conversation.

JUDY MERRIL

Basil Tomatoes à la Ipsy Wipsy

Once upon a time there was a young writer who wanted to become A Writer, and one of the very good, exciting, profitable, and educational things that happened to her in her quest was acceptance in the company of the Ipsy Wipsy Institute. Ipsy Wipsy was, in one aspect, a ChasAddams structure in Highlands, New Jersey, where high-ceilinged ballrooms and octagonal billiard rooms intersected with science fiction, poetry, history, fashion, art, and gourmet cookery in a variety of interdimensional and multidisciplinary delights, ranging from the red-on-white cocktail flag hoisted ceremoniously twice a day, to late-night solemn recitations of the Secret Ipsy Wipsy Membership Mnemonic, to hydrangea horticulture, to banquets of roast hump of buffalo in the dining hall — and steamed clams and *Basil Tomatoes* on the shore of the Shrewsbury River. In another aspect it was Fletcher and Inga Pratt and the extraordinary group of people and pageantry effects they drew together.

(The anecdotes are endless, many centering on performances of the Ipsy Wipsy Brass Band, composed of bass drum, tambourine, triangle, jew's harp, and bugle — like the time Olga Ley had a phone call from her daughter's teacher, warning her about outrageous fantasizing as a result of a show-and-tell report on the brass band reception at Ipsy Wipsy over the weekend for the Leys. But anyhow —)

Basil Tomatoes: Well, first, build a fire on the beach at the bottom of the Ipsy Wipsy terraces, and bring down the clam steamer . . .

Sorry. Basil tomatoes, present-day version, as filtered through 20 years of use by Judy Merril, and probably by now bearing no more relation to that first unbelievable taste than — well, than rereading "Baby is Three" after twenty years of living with its concepts. (I think my first experience of both was in the same year.) So —

Cut tomatoes, preferably small thin-skinned ones, preferably garden-fresh and vine-ripened, into — preferably — bite-size wedge-shapes. (You can also use slices of beefsteaks, halves of cherry tomatoes, quarters of plum tomatoes, etc. — but *preferably* as above.) Salt and pepper to taste, add an almost unnoticeable pinch of oregano, sprinkle liberally with basil, barely dampen with (pure) olive oil (if not available, leave out the oil), and just-wet-down with vinegar (I prefer malt; cider is okay; some people like tarragon). Almost everything here is flexible to some extent. I have sometimes added trace elements of curry powder and/or nutmeg-and-allspice; the oregano can, if it *must*, be commercial-ground. BUT the basil must be fresh enough (from garden or pot if at all possible, but freshly purchased in leaf form otherwise) and liberally enough used so that the finger-crumbled leaves produce a visible fresh green tracery over the tomatoes. AND the vinegar must be used in just such quantity as to produce nothing more than a damp covering on the bottom of the plate (which should be shallow and large enough to hold whatever quantity you are preparing at a density of no more than an average of two wedges' depth) when first prepared, yet "draw" enough so that there is a distinctly noticeable "juice" (not, however, covering the tomatoes) an hour or so later, in which to toss the contents just before serving.

130

SANDRA MIESEL

Bock Beer Bread

1 cup bock beer (or other dark beer)

1 package active dry yeast

3-3$\frac{1}{4}$ cups all-purpose white flour

3 tbsp. dark brown sugar, firmly packed

1 tsp. salt

1 egg, at room temperature

3 tbsp. butter or margarine, melted and cooled to room temperature

$\frac{1}{2}$ cup rye flour

Warm the beer (110°-115° F.). Sprinkle the dry yeast over it and set aside for 5 minutes to dissolve. Meanwhile combine 1 cup of white flour with rye flour. In a large mixing bowl combine sugar, salt, butter, and egg and beat until smooth. Add flour mixture and beer alternately to these ingredients, blending well. Gradually add remaining white flour, blending thoroughly after each addition. Add only enough to make a firm dough. Turn out on floured surface and knead about 10 minutes, working in only as much flour as necessary to keep dough from sticking. Finished dough should be elastic and have a "satiny" texture. Form dough into a ball, roll in a large oiled bowl so the entire ball is coated, let rise in this bowl, covered with a damp cloth, until double in bulk (about 1 hour). Punch down, form into a loaf, and place in a greased 9" x 5" x 3" loaf pan. Cover and let rise again until double in bulk. Bake in a preheated moderate oven (375° F.) for 35-40 minutes. Remove from pan and cool on a rack. A delicious accompaniment to ham or cheese.

Canadian Bacon with Onions and Apples

2-4 tbsp. butter or margarine

1 lb. Canadian bacon or ham, sliced about $\frac{1}{2}$ " thick (or cut in strips if preferred)

4 medium tart apples, peeled and thinly sliced

2 large onions, peeled, thinly sliced, and separated into rings

freshly ground black pepper (no substitute!)

Brown meat in 1 tbsp. butter and set aside. Sauté onions in the drippings, adding more butter if necessary, until transparent. Set aside with the meat. Add remaining butter to skillet and sauté apples 5-10 minutes until lightly browned but still firm. Return meat and onions to skillet, combine gently with the apples, heat through, and sprinkle *lavishly* with freshly ground black pepper. Serves four.

WALTER M. MILLER, JR.

Gopher Stew

A book of science fiction recipes should contain a few formulae for things to be cooked in a tin can in the forest after World War III. In the Southeast, one such recipe might read simply: Catch, kill, and dress one 10-12-inch gopher, and boil meat until tender, adding any available herbs such as wild garlic and sabal palmetto hearts. The "gopher" of the recipe is not a rodent but a burrowing land tortoise, *Gopherus polyphemus*, common in this region and long a part of that swampland cuisine lately called "soul food." In the summer and early fall, gophers are seen migrating across roads and through sandy clearings; when you approach, the animal's only defense is to pull himself inside his shell and batten down the hatches. Because of the shell, a slow metabolism, and a subterranean abode, the gopher should have a better resistance to radiation than most hard-to-catch game. In the winter, you will find them underground, but dig with caution; the gopher sometimes shares his hole with a southeastern diamondback.

Calculate the position of the retracted head and kill either by putting a bullet through the shell just behind this point, or by breaking through the shell with hammer, hatchet, or pointed stone, and inserting sharp knife to sever the neck. Chop all around the edges of the bottom shell plate, completely severing it from the top shell; insert a machete or long stiff butcher knife between the plate and the belly and slice the plate free. Dump the entrails, not bothering to look into the matter of reptilian giblets unless you're really starving. By now you are feeling somewhat guilty because the headless beast keeps thrashing and waving its paws as it tries to crawl away; it's not a mammal, so forget it. Reptilian meat is very persistent.

Grasp the paws with a pair of pliers and stretch them out (against their will) while you cut around behind them and free the meat from the shell. A large gopher should yield about a quart of meat, including bone. Scrub the feet thoroughly, but do not attempt to skin or declaw; part of the backwoods charm of this dish is the sight of scaly reptilian feet floating with the onions and carrots in the tomatoey goop. Treat the meat with an ordinary papayin-base tenderizer, liquid or powder, and freeze it until you find another tortoise, if one is not enough. (One does not ordinarily hunt the creatures, but encounters them while fishing, hunting, or walking in the woods.) Other types of turtle may be substituted for gopher.

1 quart tortoise meat chunks	6 hot red peppers (meat only, discard seeds)
3-4 slices bacon	3 cloves garlic
1 lb. small peeled onions	1 small can tomato sauce
4-5 carrots, sliced	half glass of sherry
4-5 small potatoes, if desired	two bay leaves, several sprigs (or a teaspoon of dry) thyme, oregano, rosemary, salt and pepper
8-9 pods of okra, sliced	
3 large, red, ripe bell peppers (or large jar pimentos)	

Fry out the bacon, then brown the gopher meat, trying not to let it jump out of the pan if recently killed (it's less active if frozen). Mince the hot pepper meat, the garlic, one of the onions, and a small carrot, and add to the browning meat, along with the herbs. Add the tomato sauce and a little water, cover tightly, and simmer until the meat is nearly tender. Add the sherry, herbs, and vegetables; cook until done. Okra is mucilaginous and has some thickening effect, but if there is too much liquid, thicken with a little brown roux or, preferably, with powdered sassafras leaves (or gumbo fillet) .

Note: the fire in hot peppers is mostly in the seeds; if you use seeds and all, use only one pepper, not six.

MICHAEL MOORCOCK
(*grace à* Hilary Moorcock)

Hillary Moorcock writes:

Moorcock is a man for traditional British fare: a small amount of the roast beef of Old England and a large amount of sliced bread, chips, baked beans (tinned), and good nice pudding to throw at the man. Cheese, peppers, anything cooked with olives, tomatoes, meat stewed in anything, wine, water, give Michael terrible headaches and bring on a huge crisis of "take this muck away." One Moorcock child is a vegetarian. One will eat nothing but beef, bloody (which she allows to drool over her chin in two streams from the corners of her mouth, the most horrific sight since Child of Dracula). Still, to a chorus of cries of "What's this foreign muck?" "You said we were having Shepherd's Pie." "Why can't we have fish and chips?" "What do you think I am — a bloody rabbit?" and "Who pays for the food anyway?" here goes. (As to the rich and famous — well, we don't invite them on condition they don't invite us. The Ballard children have often wolfed down sausage and beans Ladroke Grovienne with much appreciation. I remember Joan and Harry Harrison were sick when they returned from having dinner with us. Tom Disch ate half a turkey here one Christmas Day; Judy Merril ate the other half — there were two turkeys and John Sladek and Pamela ate nothing at all.)

Mrs. Moorcock's Famous Christmas Pudding

$\frac{1}{2}$ lb. beef suet (grated or chopped fine)

2 oz. flour

$\frac{1}{2}$ lb. raisins

$\frac{1}{4}$ mixed peel

$\frac{1}{2}$ of a grated nutmeg

$\frac{1}{2}$ oz. mixed spice

$\frac{1}{2}$ oz. mixed cinnamon

1 gill milk

1 wineglass rum or brandy

$\frac{1}{4}$ pint brown ale or Guinness

$\frac{1}{2}$ lb. *fresh* breadcrumbs

$\frac{1}{2}$ lb. sultanas

$\frac{1}{4}$ lb. currants

1 lemon, juice and chopped rind

2 oz. desiccated coconut or shredded almonds

4 eggs

pinch salt

1 grated carrot

1 grated cooking apple

Mix dry ingredients well. Beat eggs, stir in, add all liquid ingredients. Put mixture in a greased basin, seal with foil covered in a cloth so that no water can enter. Remember to allow room for the mixture to rise. Boil or steam for at least 4 to 5 hours. You can keep a pudding like this for a year or two. It is said to improve, and puddings are usually made about now (October) to give them time to ripen up for Christmas.

My favorite craze at the moment is homemade bread but I think the Christmas pudding is enough for most readers, let alone eaters, to cope with for the time being.

WARD MOORE

Kidneys — Like Father Used to Make

lamb kidneys

oil or rendered suet

red pepper

dry mustard

favorite seasoning

Split lamb kidneys lengthwise. If the butcher has been too lazy to remove the thin membrane, do so. Cover bottom of skillet with oil or rendered suet. Sauté kidneys with flat side up under low flame with cover on skillet. Season with red pepper (lightly), dry mustard, and minimum of favorite seasoning. Recover and cook until instinct tells you to turn them over.

Pea Soup — Potage Ste. Germaine

1 lb. or package split peas

3-4 good-sized carrots

fair quantity of vegetable
    oil

bell pepper

1 onion

oregano

pepper

celery, in moderation

mushrooms, optional

Fissionable Pease Porridge. Soak one pound split peas overnight in (polluted) water, enough to cover generously. Next day strain the water into good-sized pot, bring to boil, and add soaked peas. Simmer gently.

Cut three or four good-sized carrots into rounds. (The more carrots the sweeter.) Afterwards, add fair quantity of oil — olive, peanut, or safflower (cottonseed has no nutritive value); oil carries the flavor. Some cooks use animal fat but this tends to give an offensive odor, if not an offensive taste. Pepper, oregano, or other seasoning may be added at this point, *but not salt*, which should never occur while cooking as it tends to harden fibers and should only be added just before serving. Slice a good-sized onion — bell pepper in moderation, celery, or mushrooms are not excluded — and add to the hilarity. Simmer until the split peas are a total mush.

Roe Fantastic

fish roe, any variety	pepper
minced onion	ginger (optional)
soy sauce	olive oil

(General Note: Never cook with salt, it only toughens.)

It is not just shad roe which is edible: any roe can be used. (Ask any fishmonger for the roe he usually tosses away; it is not always available on the market.)

Wash the roes. Put them in a covered skillet with enough water to cover. Bring to a boil and simmer gently until the roe changes color. Remove the membrane after it has burst and discard half the broth. Add minced onion, soy sauce to taste, and pepper. Fresh ginger is optional. Add oil (olive); simmer till ready.

Tripe Provençal

2 lbs. tripe (or more if
   desired)

oregano

1 large onion

sweet basil

$\frac{1}{2}$ bell pepper, cut small

1 can tomato paste

This is perhaps more easily written than cooked. Why break your heart cutting raw tripe into squares? Throw the damn thing into boiling water and let it stew till it's soft: then it will cut easily into bite sizes.

Skim some fat off the broth and sauté a large onion in it. When onion is translucent, add a quantity of broth. Stir in a can of tomato paste. Add bell pepper, oregano, and sweet basil. Cover the tripe with this mixture, adding more broth if necessary. Simmer until thoroughly done.

LARRY NIVEN

. . . I am a good cook, but not wildly experimental. Most of my best recipes come out of the Madison Avenue Cookbook, which I heartily recommend.

So I sat and thought for quite a while, and presently remembered three original drink recipes:

Irish Coffee

I make a lot of Irish coffee. The recipe goes like this
(1) Use an Irish coffee glass, or any glass with a handle. This drink is supposed to be pretty; the glass is necessary to show it. But glass gets *hot*. You need the handle. (2) One heaping teaspoon of *brown* sugar in the glass. Follow with Irish whiskey, to taste: an ounce and a half to two ounces. You'll learn to pour by eye. (3) Fill almost to the top with *strong* black coffee, *hot*. Make it 25 percent stronger than normal. (4) Float whipped cream on top. (5) If you catch anyone trying to stir the whipped cream into the coffee, throw him the hell out. You went to a lot of trouble making that drink.

Busted Kneecap

I only made this once, in an emergency, but it worked fine. It was just after Harlan Ellison had taken a Hugo Award off me at the BayCon, and a hundred dollar side bet, all very public. I intended to get drunk.

The first party I walked into was out of everything, except a bottle of bourbon and some chunks of dry ice in the bathtub. I dropped a chunk of dry ice into the plastic glass and poured bourbon over it.

It was spectacular! It boiled and bubbled and smoked cold smoke that drifted over my hand and toward the floor. By and by it got less active as water ice partially surrounded the frozen CO_2. The water was freezing out of the bourbon, leaving me with concentrated, carbonated bourbon at about 20° below. One has to sip this drink carefully, and it will still numb one's mouth. But it got me very drunk indeed, and did me no permanent harm.

It was still smoking dangerously when Harlan walked in. I tried to hand it to him and he jumped back about four feet, screaming, "Don't tell me this guy doesn't hold a grudge!"

[Warning: this drink may be hazardous to one's lips, mouth, and/or throat. — ED.]

Dry Martini

Dry Martini consists of absolute alcohol (ethyl alcohol, 100%) with sodium in it. Add water, you get pyrotechnics and *more alcohol.* Add vermouth, you get the same result with some slight flavoring. NOT RECOMMENDED FOR HUMAN BEINGS. The inventor, Russel Seitz, tells me that it should be sipped not gulped.

[You have been warned. — ED.]

ALAN E. NOURSE

(Note to Ed.: This recipe was rejected by *Sunset* magazine's Outdoor Cookery editor as unsuitable for a family magazine. — AEN)

North Pacific Dungeness Crab with Bourbon

one Pacific Northwest beach

8 medium to large fresh-caught Dungeness crab, males only

one clean 5-gallon can

4 gallons sea water

one driftwood beach fire

2 bottles good sour-mash bourbon

8 Excedrin tablets

one driftwood board 5 feet long

Build good, roaring beach fire. Fill can with sea water, place on fire, bring to rolling boil. Throw in live crab (don't watch if this sort of thing bothers you) and boil for 10 minutes. Then dump water onto beach, preferably without putting out fire, and lay the crab out on driftwood board to cool enough to clean. Slosh off the cleaned crab in fresh sea water. Pick and eat crab with fingers while still warm, interspersed with liberal drafts (bad word, make it "draughts") of bourbon. The more crab you eat the better the bourbon tastes, and the more bourbon you drink the better the crab tastes.

Serves 4.

NOTE: It is recommended strongly that you build your fire and do your eating *above* the high-tide line, with reference to local tide tables, because once you sit down to eat you may well not get up again before morning. Keep Excedrin in a cool, dry place, also above the high-tide line, to provide surcease the following day. Crab shells may be thrown back into the drink at any time; dust to dust returneth and all that.

RACHEL C. PAYES

Angel Goop Cake Roll

any angel food cake mix

Prepare angel food cake mix as directed and bake half of the batter in a jelly-roll pan lined with waxed paper. Bake at 375° F. for 15 minutes. Immediately loosen edges; turn upside down on towel (clean) sprinkled with 10X (Confectioners') Sugar. Roll cake and towel from narrow end. Cool. Unroll. Spread with $\frac{2}{3}$ of the Filling Goop, reroll without towel, spread remaining Goop on top and chill for 3 hours. (Other half of batter can be baked as an extra cake roll or in a loaf pan.)

Filling:

1 can blueberry pie filling

$\frac{1}{2}$ cup chopped nuts (whatever's available but I think peanuts would be dreadful)

2 tbsp. frozen concentrated orange juice

1 can vanilla pudding (or a cup of Cool'n'Creamy)

$\frac{1}{2}$ cup shredded coconut

1 cup prepared whipped topping (Dream Whip or whatever)

Mix everything except whipped topping, then fold it in. You can use cherry pudding instead of blueberry filling.

145

JOHN T. PHILLIFENT

Utility of B1 Deficiency

Here is a peculiarity of my own. It isn't a recipe exactly. It is
in all probability me. I will gist here what took me a long time to
find out: that my normal diet contains very little of the usual
food-sources for Vitamin "B." Bee-one, that is. And one of the
side-effects of a B1 deficiency is a tendency to nightmare, even
to the point of halluciantions (I'm not going to alter that . . . it
looks as if it meant something weird). I don't have trouble with
nightmares, but I do have a fairly wild imagination, and I can
throw a hallucination any time . . . remaining fully aware of it . . .
something like an LSD trip. I discovered the connection some
time ago when I was prescribed a tonic after a bad bout of
influenza. It was loaded with yeast, among other things. I have
since tried it under hard control conditions, enough to prove —
to me anyway, and *for* me — that if I ingest adequate amounts of
B1 I can't think of a thing to write about. The imagination just
gets grounded. And that's it, for what it may be worth. Cut down
on the cereals, liver, and bacon and eggs (now there's an unimagi-
native dish for you!), avoid yeast in any form, and in a week or
two you'll be seeing visions . . . and maybe writing them down,
too!

[As John T. points out, this is his own thing. It is not
recommended for anybody else whatsoever. You have been
warned. — ED.]

146

JOE F. PUMILIA

Tortilla Saucer

2 packaged tortillas
1 can Spanish rice

salt, butter, chili, etc., all optional

Good for camping or quick snacks between short stories. Take two tortillas out of the package (unless you have a flat rock and hanker to make your own) and heat by putting directly on stove burner (or grill, if camping). Keep on the flame for several seconds and remove with your hand, fast so you don't get burned. Take Spanish rice right out of the can (unless you know how to prepare it, which I don't) and spoon onto a tortilla; put other tortilla on top, making a sort of circular floppy sandwich. If fastidious, you can heat the rice, but it takes longer. Preparation time: about 45 seconds. Connoisseurs can add salt to the rice, and butter, chili, etc. Properly prepared, the Tortilla Saucer should cause a Mexican to stare in puzzlement and ask, *"¿Que es esto?"*

ROBERT RAY

Casserole Corwen

[This we heartily ate when visiting the Rays in their lovely Welsh valley after the Eastercon at Worcester, England. — ED.]

1 package shell macaroni

1 small onion, finely chopped

6-8 rashers bacon, chopped

1 small tub cottage cheese

1 cup grated Parmesan cheese

$\frac{1}{2}$ green pepper, finely chopped

Prepare shell macaroni according to instructions. While this is cooking, sauté bacon, onion, green pepper, and reserve.

As soon as macaroni is done, add cottage cheese and the reserved onion-pepper-bacon. Toss to mix well. Top with grated Parmesan cheese and serve immediately to the hungry. Serves 6-8 well.

Potato Casserole Ray

2 lbs. potatoes, parboiled, then sliced thinly

6-8 hardboiled eggs

2 green peppers, veined, seeded, and sliced

6 sausages, fried in lard and sliced endwise

2-3 onions, sliced thinly

$\frac{1}{2}$ cup grated cheese (hard type)

In a greased casserole place a layer of the thinly sliced parboiled potatoes. Then a layer of green pepper, more potato, onions, potato, hardboiled eggs sliced, potato, sausage, and a final layer of potato over which spread a cheese (Parmesan, Cheddar, one of the harder cheeses which grates easily). Dot with butter. Bake at 450° F. about $\frac{1}{2}$ hour until tender. This also eats like more and was served to us with a Raspberry Fool. One can vary the layers as the larder permits but the result is a marvelous blending of vegetable flavors and meat.

ALLEN RIVERS

Poor Man's Pepper Steak

$\frac{3}{4}$ lb. ground beef

cooking oil to coat skillet

$\frac{1}{3}$ cup Italian flavored
bread crumbs

1 large green pepper

1 bouillon cube and 1
cup water

$\frac{1}{4}$ cup milk

$\frac{1}{3}$ can Hunt's tomato herb
sauce

salt and pepper to taste

3 cups (cooked) large
elbow macaroni

small amount of flour

Combine ground beef, bread crumbs, milk, salt and pepper, mix well, and roll into meatballs about 1 inch in diameter. Roll in flour, then brown in cooking oil. Add green pepper, cut into $\frac{3}{4}$-inch strips. Add extra flour if a thicker sauce is desired. Dissolve bouillon cube in one cup hot water, and add bouillon and tomato sauce, pouring them over meatballs. Stir, cover, lower flame, and let simmer for one hour. Add macaroni, simmer five minutes more, and serve.

JOANNA RUSS

The following are the only two recipes I know that are mine own. One I made up; one is traditional wisdom from a friend.

Hamburger and Stewed Tomatoes

1 lb. hamburger
1 medium-sized can of stewed
    tomatoes-with-onion-and-whatnot

Combine one pound of hamburger and one medium-sized can (regular size) of stewed tomatoes-with-onion-and-whatnot. Boil (simmer, that is) until the hamburger is done. It might be a little watery. You might also want to skim off the fat, depending on how fatty the meat was. I forgot: pull the hamburger meat into pieces before you empty it into the saucepan with the stewed tomatoes. Very quick recipe.

A Large Salad for a Party

1 head cauliflower (large)

2 lbs. string beans

box cherry tomatoes

oil and vinegar dressing
(to taste)

Steal one head of cauliflower (large) from a friend's garden, or two medium-sized heads. Also steal (this is how I did it) about

151

two pounds of string beans. [You could probably buy them as long as you're sure they're fresh. — ED.] Boil both (separately) until done. Drain both. Cut the cauliflower (or rend apart by hand) into pieces $1\frac{1}{2}$ " or so across. Put the whole mess into a large bowl and add oil-and-vinegar dressing with whatever flavorings you like. Marinate in the refrigerator for a day. Then drain off the dressing just before the party; put it in some superfluous dish or other to serve with the salad. At the last minute add a box or so of cherry tomatoes.

I actually *made up* this salad for a party one summer, dazzling myself with my ingenuity and serving 6 people. (It would really serve about 8-10.) A lot of people took portions home.

Shrimp, Quick and Good

My mother used to use concentrated mushroom soup from a can (without diluting it) with boiled shrimp and rice. I doubt if this constitutes a real recipe but it, too, was quick and tasted good.

JOSEPHINE SAXTON

Commemoration Salad

Here is a "secret" recipe — secret because I have no business to tell it, especially in writing, but as I have already done so in *Vector for Seven* I may as well do it again. It's a recipe for a very powerful salad, invented by George Ivanovitch Gurdjieff, and eaten annually at the commemoration feast which his disciples still hold. I did the cooking for twenty or more people for a while at one of those groups, and it was there that I learned how to make it by observing and tasting and smelling — the recipe was never meant to be written down, but to my immense pride I was told once that I was the only one who could make it so that it had its authentic flavor as it had been eaten "in the old days" of Paris. This was of course a mixed compliment, for the key to a correct result is that the salad should have a taste strongly reminiscent of fresh varnish. Please note that it was invented before the days of polyurethane. It is an excellent starter to a meal, more especially one of strongly individual flavors, for it cleanses both the palate and the mind of everything except itself and should be accompanied by several glasses of Armagnac — all very strange to gourmets, no doubt, but Mr. Gurdjieff rarely if ever did things in a "normal" fashion. The quantities are not fixed, but if you put in equal quantities of all the vegetables and have sufficient liquid to nicely cover without it being too wet, you will not be far wrong. So:

153

Finely chopped:

celery	apples
cucumber	parsley
radishes	tomatoes
mint (fresh)	spring onions
red peppers	garlic
green peppers	

is blended into thick tomato juice *seasoned with:*

paprika	salt
powdered mustard	black pepper

and diluted with:

wine vinegar	olive oil

Further cloves of garlic are added, finely crushed rather than chopped.

It must be left overnight, and well covered, too, for obvious reasons. Half a teacupful is a usual serving. Please do not think that if it is correctly prepared it will harm your health — I have never known it to do so. I know a man who used to have an ulcer and who when faced with a portion of this knew he should certainly refuse it; but he was too brave and polite to do so, and went on to a third helping and felt not the slightest pang afterwards. But I speak of miracles; you must judge for yourselves! You see, although I give no exact quantity for the mustard and garlic, I do mean a *lot* in proportion to the other ingredients.

154

Balkan Salad with Shrimp

I have another starter salad which I invented myself, and this too is of a Balkan ilk. Similarly, I give no precise quantities:

chicken stock	pepper, fresh
yogurt	sea salt, optional
cucumber, diced	lemon juice
radishes, sliced	parsley, finely cut
prawns or shrimp	paprika, chives, and
chives, chopped	parsley for garnish

This is a much milder and more delicate dish than the Gurdjieff Commemorative.

First have some strong chicken stock and let it cool; put about one part stock to two parts good goatsmilk yogurt and add to that some diced cucumber, sliced radishes, chopped chives, a little fresh black pepper, a touch of sea salt if your stock was plain, some finely cut parsley, a good squeeze of fresh lemon juice, and some whole prawns or shrimp. Mix well and serve well chilled with a sprinkle of paprika and chives and parsley on top of each portion.

Haphazard Crossbreed Soup

Speaking of starters to meals reminds me of a much plainer soup that I invented, it being a kind of haphazard crossbreed between potato and leek soup, but this is always served hot.

1 lb. leeks	parsley
1 large potato	pepper
chicken stock	milk

155

I half-inch and wash a pound of leeks and dice a large potato (in England a large potato is perhaps four inches long; I have never been to Idaho . . .) and cook them both until tender in three-quarters of a pint of chicken stock with a bit of parsley and a grind of pepper. When it has cooled I liquidize it in the blender and adjust its consistency and flavor with milk and chicken stock, if necessary. It is a beautiful pale green and you should serve it with a spiral of fresh cream floating on each dish, after gently heating it.

Fiddly Prawns and Mussels

And then there is another soup that I don't make very often because it is fiddly to make and rather expensive, but it has always been so vastly appreciated.

$\frac{1}{2}$ lb. cooked prawns	parsley, chopped
$\frac{1}{4}$ lb. prawn shells	sliver of garlic
two cloves	pepper
white wine	cream
a butter roux	$\frac{1}{2}$ lemon
mussels	hot red pepper
chicken stock	onion
$\frac{1}{2}$ lb. white fish	oysters, optional
a bay leaf	clams, optional

Take the shells from half a pound of large cooked prawns and simmer *half* of the discarded material in chicken stock for about fifteen minutes, then pound and liquidize them and strain them into another pan containing some plain white fish (about half a pound would do) and a bay leaf, some chopped parsley to taste, grind of black pepper, a half lemon with two cloves in it, and sufficient dry white wine to simmer the fish in for five minutes. Discard the lemon and bay leaf and pick out any bones and then liquidize the mixture again. Thicken it with a butter roux and serve it with the prawns in it plus some freshly boiled mussels (they will have been cooking meanwhile; you could have scrubbed and bearded them first, and don't forget the onion and sliver of garlic in their pan) and a spiral of thick whipped double cream and some very small bits of hot red pepper. Rich people could put in instead of or as well as the mussels some oysters and clams, but I think they should be fresh so I have never used clams; I have never found fresh ones in England, and oysters cost a *bomb*.

Olde English Pease Pudding, or A Tantra Version of Indian Dahl

And then for the days when the English fogs close in and we have no money for fancy dishes, I sometimes make my own version of pease pudding; and just as it indicates in the nursery rhyme it's nice cold, too!

bacon ribs (pork spareribs)	$\frac{1}{2}$ lb. yellow split peas (lentils)
onion, chopped	Northumbrian folk-song, optional
black pepper	

Tantra version:

olive oil

hot spices

Obtain some bacon ribs (pork spareribs) and simmer them, cut and snapped, in a large pan with a chopped onion, a little black pepper, and *no salt*. If you suspect that your ribs are very salty, then blanch them and throw out the water first. Add a half-pound of yellow split peas and just simmer it very slowly for a very long time, stirring occasionally and preferably singing a Northumbrian folk-song, although this is not essential. In the fullness of time the pan will contain a thick mush, which will stick to the bottom of the pan unless you scrape assiduously and then cool to extract the bones. The meat will have left the bones, and you shred it and put it back with the lentil mush. You can eat this just as it is, and it is truly delicious, or you can reheat it in the oven in rather a lot of good olive oil, where it will become a Tantra version of Indian Dahl, especially if you first mix hot spices into the lentil mix. I say Tantra because they are not vegetarians and would permit bacon flavoring. Olde English Pease Pudding or Indian Dahl, it comes to the same thing — one is irresistibly drawn towards indigestion unless great self-control is exercised! Yummy.

A Note on Chips

P.S. Chips just are not chips without vinegar! It's the smell of hot vinegar on cold English nights which has drawn me half a mile on a full stomach to partake; it's a mystical experience. Call 'em French Fries if you like — I know what we call crisps are chips to you — but honey, it's chips. God, I think I'll go down to the chippy and get some . . .

JAMES SCHMITZ

Two-Stage Lentil Soup

One of our cold weather favorites, developed and refined over a number of years. It takes some effort, and it's not a cheap dish when you tote it all up; but we rate it as one of the world's great din-dins.

Note for those unfamiliar with present-day lentils: There was a time when you soaked lentils overnight and then cooked them half the day to get them soft enough to eat, and many cookbooks still tell you to do this. Now, however, because growers have developed new strains of lentils or because they process them before packaging, lentils cook very quickly, and the main trick is to stop cooking them before they turn into a mush, euphemistically referred to as a puree after it's been mashed through a strainer. All the lentil soup recipes I've seen call for a mush, but here we want them to keep their shape. It adds a good bit to the flavor and appearance of the soup.

So know your lentils before you start. Brands vary, and if you're using an unfamiliar one, do a trial run by dropping a few spoonfuls into barely simmering water and checking the cooking time. The brand I use, called Golden Grain, is done in thirty to thirty-five minutes, overdone less than five minutes later.

The first stage of the soup is done one day, the second stage the next day, to make it easy on the cook.

First-stage ingredients:

9 cups of cold water

1 sizable lean smoked ham hock, cut into three or four pieces

cut-up sections of beef marrow bones (If not available, plain soup bones can be substituted.)

1 medium onion, quartered

6 medium carrots, cut into large chunks

6 medium celery stalks, ditto (Don't use the leaves here.)

$1\frac{1}{2}$ tbsp. Accent

five grinds or so of black pepper

It's worth getting your ham hock from a good delicatessen. The ones found in supermarkets are generally lousy. Medium carrots means carrots that don't measure much more than an inch across the wide end. If in doubt, use fewer carrots rather than more. With the onion and celery, the exact quantity isn't too important.

Method:

Put the hock and bones into water. If nine cups don't cover them, add more. Bring to a boil, reduce to slow simmer — just a few bubbles coming up here and there. After ten minutes, take out the beef marrow bones, if any, scoop out the marrow and put it in refrigerator. It will go back into the soup at the end. Return bones to the water. Add two to three tablespoons of vinegar.

Don't skim off the gathering scum, as many recipes recommend. It's loaded with vitamins and minerals, adds flavor, and will soon be reabsorbed if left alone.

Simmer on gently for a minimum of two hours, which is good enough, though four or five hours won't hurt at all. Keep up the water level, using simmering-hot water to refill. At the end of this period, add in the chopped vegetables, the Accent (or other monosodium glutamate), and the pepper. Don't add salt. Simmer another two hours — no more. Strain out the solids. You now have your soup stock. Cool and store in quart glass jars, or the like, in the refrigerator.

Discard the stock vegetables and bones. If in a thrifty mood, as I sometimes am, you can keep the ham. The lean parts are good protein, and served with a horseradish or mustard sauce, or mixed with chopped onion and fried as meat balls, they're edible. But frankly, the hock has blown most of its flavor by then. And it's served its purpose.

Second-stage ingredients:

- $\frac{1}{2}$ medium onion, finely diced
- 3 medium carrots, sliced very thin
- 3 medium celery stalks, ditto (no leaves)
- 8-pack of Oscar Meyer's Smokies (Other good sausages can be substituted, but the Smokies are great in the soup.)

- the marrow you scooped out of the bones the day before
- 2 cups lentils

Method:

Next day, take the stock out of the refrigerator, remove the fat collected on top. Start heating the stock. Brown the Smokies with a bit of butter. While they're browning, cut up the vegetables as indicated. Cut up the browned Smokies, using kitchen scissors and paper towel to hold them, into half-inch slices. Add them, the vegetables, and cut-up pieces of marrow to the stock. Simmer gently for twenty minutes. Don't add more water. While the soup's simmering, wash the lentils thoroughly in pan or strainer and remove any black lentils or other odd objects you notice. Add to soup after twenty minutes.

This is the crucial period. Keep the heat down, simmer gently, stir the soup up from time to time to keep the lentils well mixed; and toward the end of the cooking period you've established, sample the lentils frequently until they get to the point where they're quite soft but still intact. The soup can go from the perfect stage to something less in around three minutes.

Cool quickly by putting the container in the kitchen sink and surrounding it with cold water, stirring frequently. Replace the water as it warms up. Then put the soup in the refrigerator until serving time. Reheat gently, and serve with the kind of rather coarse gray bread referred to variously as Russian, Bavarian, or Bohemian pumpernickel. Not the brown kind. Plus unsalted butter.

This makes a complete meal for six people. As a leftover, the soup can be reheated two or three times without losing much flavor.

BOB SHAW

Deadline Stew

My wife refuses to be associated with this recipe in any way, but it is one I invented to meet a specific need — that of the author working alone, who needs solid tasty nourishment but has no time to prepare elaborate dishes.

Ingredients:

1 lb. of sausages (pork, beef, or mixed)

2 cups of water

2 medium-to-large onions

2 Oxo cubes

2 medium potatoes

seasoning

Method:

Heat the water in a pan and dissolve the Oxo cubes in it. Cut the sausages up into pieces about $1\frac{1}{2}$ inches long, then finely chop the onions and potatoes, and put the lot into the pan. Season to taste and simmer slowly, with an occasional stir, for at least thirty minutes.

As a variation, you can leave out the potatoes, but before serving stir in a small packet of instant potato to thicken the stew.

[Sadie Shaw associates herself with the following recipe. — ED.]

163

Martian Madness

Ingredients:

1 lb. digestive biscuits
$\frac{1}{2}$ lb. margarine
2 oz. butter
3 oz. brown sugar
2 tbsps. drinking chocolate
2 tbsps. golden syrup

1 measure dark rum
1 to 2 oz. glacé cherries
cake-decorating beads, or small quantity of icing
baking chocolate

Method:

Put margarine, butter, brown sugar, drinking chocolate, and syrup into saucepan and melt slowly, stirring well. Crush the biscuits and add to mixture in pan. Stir again and pour into greased baking tray, then roll out flat. Sprinkle rum over mixture, then cover with melted baking chocolate. Before confection has set, decorate by pressing in glacé cherries (representing Mars, the red planet) at regular spacing, and beside each put two small beads or blobs of icing to represent Mars' two moons. When mixture has fully set, cut into squares with one cherry on each.

Note: This confection is called Martian Madness because it is crazy to eat a lot of it if you are trying to lose weight. Of course, it was designed for eating on Mars, where the fractional gravity means that even the most solidly built person has no weight problems.

[Sadie calls for "digestive biscuits," which means digestive cookies. These are obtainable in most American supermarkets now, for Peake-Freen and others are exporting digestive biscuits. I think any running under that name would do nicely. They're basically a dry, not overly sweet cookie — like an arrowroot or possibly graham cracker. I suppose graham crackers could be used as a substitute, failing anything imported. — ED.]

T. L. SHERRED

Yeah, I cook once in a while. Being a bachelor, I use every shortcut for later dishwashing I can think of. I eat this one every couple of weeks or so.

Sirloin Tips

2 tbsps. cooking oil

2 lbs. round steak (It's cheaper than sirloin, and dosed well with meat tenderizer it works just as well. Cut it up small.)

1 can beef consommé (Campbell's soup; $10\frac{1}{2}$-oz. can)

1 cup cheap Burgundy wine (I use A&P's brand, but the cheaper the better.)

$\frac{1}{4}$ tsp. onion salt

2 tsps. Chinese soy sauce

2 tbsps. cornstarch

$\frac{1}{4}$ tsp. garlic salt (If you like garlic. I don't use it.)

Brown the meat in the fat. If you use a three- or four-quart kettle instead of a frying pan, you have only one pan to wash. Stir in the consommé, wine, soy sauce, and the salt. Heat to a boil and simmer slowly for an hour.

Blend cornstarch with another $\frac{1}{2}$ cup of wine and stir into the meat mixture. Stir until the whole mess thickens and boils. Boil about a minute and stir steadily. Then pour it over rice — and noodles work, too.

If it seems too thick, add some more wine to suit yourself. A bottle of cheap Burgundy is less than 95¢. For the rice, I use the minute or instant-type rice. I'm trying to find a way where I don't have to wash the second kettle.

ROBERT SILVERBERG

Robert Silverberg's Beefsteak Tartare

1 lb. raw chopped meat (serves two)

1 raw egg (out of shell)

1 small onion, 1 clove garlic, both minced

oregano, Coleman's mustard (dry), Tabasco sauce, chili
powder (hot), Worcestershire sauce, salt, pepper (freshly
ground), sharp paprika, green peppercorns (whole),
other hot stuff, to taste

Smooge everything around until thoroughly mixed. Garnish
with anchovies and capers. Serve chilled.

Barbara Silverberg's
Martian Salad Dressing

1 clove garlic

1 cup sour cream

2 tsp. mayonnaise

salt and pepper

1 cup fresh sorrel leaves

8 freshly picked basil
leaves

Dump into blender and puree till speckled and smooth.
Serves 4-6.

Barbara Silverberg's Raspberry-Madeira Bavarian Cream

2 packages frozen
  raspberries, thawed

$\frac{2}{3}$ cup Madeira

1 cup heavy cream

1 envelope gelatin

Drain frozen raspberries, reserve 1 cup of juice. Stir gelatin into $\frac{1}{4}$ cup raspberry juice. Heat remaining juice to boiling, add gelatin mixture. Stir till gelatin is completely dissolved. Cool. Add Madeira. Refrigerate till mixture begins to set but is still liquid (20-30 minutes) . Meanwhile, whip cream till stiff. When gelatin mixture is ready combine it with whipped cream. Refrigerate for 15 minutes. Then fold in drained raspberries. Chill in individual bowls or 2-quart oiled mold for several hours.

Serves 6.

KATHLEEN SKY

Sauerbraten

3 lbs. beef (roundsteak cut up like stewmeat is very good, but almost any cubed beef will do)

garlic (optional)

2 tsps. salt, pepper

2 cups vinegar (red wine vinegar is best)

2 cups water

$\frac{1}{2}$ cup sliced onion (about one medium onion)

2 bay leaves

$\frac{1}{4}$ cup sugar

shortening and bit of flour for browning meat

sour cream

egg noodles

dried parsley

Rub cubes of meat with cut surface of garlic (if desired). Salt and pepper meat and place in large shallow pan one layer deep. (Bottom of roaster pan is good for this.) Heat vinegar, water, onion, bay leaves, and sugar together. DO NOT BOIL. Pour hot mixture over meat. Cover. Let stand in refrigerator for 4 to 8 days (6-day sauerbraten is best for most people not used to it). Turn meat cubes in mixture once a day. At end of soaking time, drain the meat, saving the liquid. Flour the meat lightly and brown in fat. Take out the onions and the bay leaves from the liquid and pour half of it over the meat. Cover the pan and SIMMER until tender — maybe two hours or so. Add more of the liquid as required to keep about $\frac{1}{2}$ inch of liquid in the pan. Drain off the liquid left and serve the sauerbraten over egg noodles. Sprinkle the sour cream with parsley and heap it over the meat and noodles.

Serves 6.

JOHN SLADEK

I've been checking the old family recipe book and have found the following, which might be useful to the starving:

Caligula Salad with Muttered Dressing

Caligula Salad:

lettuce

(tomatoes are optional)

Muttered Dressing:

2 hard-boiled eggs

pinch of mustard (dry mustard)

1 tsp. bacon grease or salad oil

2 tbsps. Worcestershire sauce

2 tbsps. cider vinegar

$\frac{1}{4}$ tsp. sugar

salt and pepper

Mash egg yolks and mix with mustard, pepper, salt, and sugar. Stir in oil gradually, then sauce and vinegar. Mix in finely chopped egg whites and, if desired, crumbled crisp bacon.

Accursed Steak Pie

(Note: It is said that James II was so taken with this dish that he drew his sword and on the spot created it Duchess of Williamsborough. His successor revoked the title and ordered the luckless pie to be imprisoned in the Tower, guarded by yeomen called "beefeaters.")

For the filling:

$1\frac{1}{2}$ lbs beef, cut in cubes

2 or 3 slices of bacon

1 onion

1 boiled potato

2 hard-boiled eggs

1 tbsp. lard

1 tbsp. Worcestershire sauce

salt and pepper

For the pastry:

$1\frac{1}{2}$ cups flour

1 cup margarine or butter

$\frac{1}{2}$ tsp. salt

lemon juice

Make the pastry first. Sift flour and salt together, add the butter, cut into small cubes. To some cold water add a squeeze of lemon juice. Use barely enough of this to stick the dough together, and mix. Roll on a floured surface to the thickness of $\frac{1}{2}$ inch. Brush off all loose flour. Fold in thirds, like a business letter, then fold this up into a square. Roll out, fold again. Refrigerate for 20 minutes. Repeat the fold-roll-fold business. Refrigerate for another 20 minutes. Repeat again, and refrigerate until ready to roll out and use.

Fry the bacon; remove to a deep pie tin. Season beef with salt and pepper, brown it, remove to pie tin. Lightly brown the onion and boiled potato (sliced); add these to beef and bacon. Put beef stock in a frying pan and add spices, sauce, salt, sugar. Boil and thicken with flour. Pour this gravy over the other stuff, top with slices of egg, and cover with pastry. Bake first in a hot oven (450° F.) for ten minutes, then reduce heat to 300° F. and continue, for one hour's total baking time.

Fountain Pen Stew

1 chicken	1 large can tomatoes
1 lb. carrots	2 chicken-stock cubes
2 lbs. potatoes	1 bouquet garni
$\frac{1}{2}$ lb. mushrooms	1 pinch rosemary
2 green peppers or $\frac{1}{2}$ lb.	(optional)
okra	salt and pepper to taste
2 large onions	butter, flour

Slice onion and fry it in a little butter until golden. Put it in large casserole. Clean and quarter chicken and add it to the casserole with all the raw vegetables, chopped into stew-sized chunks. Make the stock cubes into $\frac{1}{2}$ pint of boiling stock. Add this, the tomatoes, and all the seasoning and cook in a 300° F. oven for $1\frac{1}{2}$ to 2 hours.

To thicken it, make a paste of 2 parts butter and 1 part flour. A tablespoon or two of this paste should be enough: stir it into the stew and return to the oven for 10 minutes.

(Note: Some might prefer to replace the chicken with four large fountain pens. This alters the flavor.)

Chocolate Tart à la Shirt Factory

6 tbsp. flour

10 tbsp. castor sugar (in U.S., $\frac{5}{8}$ cup canning sugar. At least I think it's called canning sugar. Anyway, fine sugar.)

$\frac{1}{4}$ lb. butter

2 eggs

$\frac{1}{2}$ lb. bittersweet chocolate

2 tsp. instant coffee

$\frac{1}{2}$ cup chopped nuts (optional)

icing sugar (U.S., powdered sugar)

Melt butter and chocolate in a double boiler. Add sugar and coffee. Beat in eggs, then stir in flour. Stir in nuts. Pour into well-greased cake pan (the kind with the removable bottom comes in handy here). Bake at 400° F. for 12 to 15 minutes. The tart should, like brownies, be cake-like at the edges and fudge-like in the middle. When cool, dust with icing sugar. Unlike some cakes, this ages well, and it's best when served a few days after baking. Serve with whipped cream. Invite your friends from the shirt factory.

IDELLA PURNELL STONE

Virginia Goober Cookies

Cream together:

$\frac{1}{3}$ cup peanut butter $\frac{1}{2}$ cup white sugar

$\frac{1}{2}$ cup shortening $\frac{1}{2}$ tsp. salt

$\frac{1}{2}$ cup brown sugar

Then add:

1 egg   1 tsp. soda

1 tsp. vanilla $1\frac{1}{2}$ cups sifted flour

1 tsp. cinnamon

Mix well. Shape into marbles. Place on well-greased cookie sheet, flatten with fork tines: bake at 375° F. for 12-15 minutes (depends on size of marbles). Do not let become too brown.

Favorite Potato Salad

8-10 large potatoes   1 tsp. dry mustard

5-6 hard-cooked eggs   2 tsp. salt

1 tsp. cumin seed (whole) $\frac{1}{4}$ tsp. pepper

$\frac{1}{2}$ cup vinegar   *(more)*

176

$\frac{1}{2}$ cup olive oil

$\frac{1}{8}$ cup soy sauce

2 large brown onions

2-4 cups celery

Thoroughly boil 8-10 large potatoes. Peel and cube. Cool slightly. Add 5-6 hard-cooked eggs, diced; add cumin, vinegar with which is mixed the dry mustard, salt, and pepper. Then add olive oil and soy sauce. Mix thoroughly in salad. Add two large onions, peeled and minced, celery (leaves and all chopped fine), and mix again. Taste and correct seasoning. If too dry, add some commercial mayonnaise. Or sour cream. Optional seasonings: a tsp. chili powder with the other powders; 1 cup unpeeled radishes, sliced thin (nice touch of color); 1-2 cups unpeeled cucumbers, cubed; 5-6 slices crisp crumbled bacon; $\frac{1}{2}$ cup finely minced parsley. Serve in large bowl with paprika over top and sprigs of parsley for garnish.

Shish Kebab

3 lbs. lamb shoulder, boned and cubed 1" square

3-4 large onions, cut into eighths

4-5 large peppers in 1" squares

5 semi-ripe medium-sized tomatoes, cut into 4 or 5 pieces each

small mushrooms, brushed with olive oil

strips of bacon in 2" squares

3 cloves garlic

1 tbsp. salt

1 large can tomato juice

1 cup claret (optional)

$\frac{1}{4}$ cup olive oil

$\frac{1}{2}$ tsp. oregano

$\frac{1}{2}$ tsp. rosemary

Have butcher bone and cut lamb shoulder into cubes about an inch square. Ask him for bones and trimmings with the meat. Prepare a marinade of the garlic, rubbed to a paste with 1 tbsp. salt; add tomato juice, claret, olive oil, oregano, and rosemary. Let cubed lamb stand in this till following day (if hurried, 2-3 hours will do). Stir a few times during soaking.

Now peel onions, cut into eighths; de-vein and seed peppers and cut into inch-square pieces; cut semi-ripe medium-sized tomatoes into four or five pieces; if you like small mushrooms, have them, brushed with olive oil; cut strips of raw bacon into two-inch pieces.

Thread on skewers (if you don't have any, your butcher does) one each of ingredients, including, of course, lamb; repeat till skewer is full; leave tiny space between each bite. Have broiler at 450° F.

Place skewers on rack in pan under broiler about two inches from flame. Watch carefully. Just barely burn a few edges of onion and bacon, then remove pan, turn skewers over, and broil the other side. Or cook over coals.

Serve at once with tossed green salad, and tiny hot biscuits with butter.

Buttermilk Soup

(For hot weather and for reducing diets.)

1 quart buttermilk	$\frac{1}{2}$ cup finely minced parsley
1 cup green onion	
1 cup peeled diced cucumber	salt and pepper to taste

To one quart good buttermilk, add one cup onion, chopped small (use most of the green tops, too), finely minced parsley (omit stems), one cup peeled cucumber, and salt and pepper to taste. Chill at least three hours. I don't like buttermilk, but find this soup delightful.

Cheese Soup

$\frac{1}{2}$ lb. bacon

1 4-oz can pimentos

$\frac{1}{2}$ to 1 lb. Cheddar cheese, cubed

1 large can (#$2\frac{1}{2}$) tomatoes, well crushed

1 or 2 large onions

In a large pot, fry about $\frac{1}{2}$ lb. bacon; remove bacon. Mince 1 or 2 large onions and brown in bacon fat; add 1 large can tomatoes, well crushed, and can of pimentos cut in strips. Simmer 15 minutes. Just before removing from fire, add 1 to 2 cups hot water, bring to boil again, add $\frac{1}{2}$ to 1 lb. Cheddar cheese in small cubes. Crumble bacon and add to soup. Serve piping hot with crisp French bread.

Spoon Bread

(I always triple this recipe!)

$\frac{1}{2}$ cup yellow cornmeal

2 tsp. baking powder

1 cup milk

1 cup cooked rice (optional)

$\frac{1}{8}$ lb. butter

2 egg whites, stiff

1 tsp. salt

2 egg yolks, creamy

In double-boiler top, over boiling water, place cornmeal and milk; stir till it thickens. Remove. Stir in butter, salt, baking powder, rice. Whip egg whites until stiff and yolks separately till creamy; stir yolks into cooled cornmeal mixture, fold whites in carefully.

Pour into well-buttered baking dish. Bake at 350° F. about $\frac{1}{2}$ hour. When recipe is tripled, it usually requires a longer baking time; however, this depends on size of pans. After about twenty minutes, one may peek cautiously! When browned on top, it is usually done . . . but this is soufflé-ish and will fall if not quite done, so a few more minutes do not hurt. Serve hot with plenty of butter.

Stuffed Peppers

8-10 green peppers
$\frac{1}{2}$ lb. ground beef
$\frac{1}{2}$ lb. ground pork
1 tsp. salt
$\frac{1}{4}$ tsp. pepper
1 small minced onion
1 large chopped tomato

$\frac{1}{2}$ tsp. cumin seed
2 tbsp. sesame seed
2-3 egg whites stiffly beaten
2-3 egg yolks
2-3 tbsp. flour

Prepare green peppers by taking off caps and removing seeds; parboil about 10 minutes. Fill with ground beef and pork, mixed with salt, pepper, onion, chopped tomato, cumin, and sesame seed. Place peppers in well-greased baking dish. Place filling in loosely.

Beat 2-3 egg whites till very stiff; still beating, add yolks slowly, one at a time, then 1 tbsp. flour for each egg, slowly. Carefully bathe each pepper with this egg batter, and cook $\frac{3}{4}$ to 1 hour in a moderate 350° F. oven.

E. C. TUBB

Orange Wine

Most country wines are a bugbear to make because of the tedious preparation; however, this is one that can be made with a minimum of equipment, effort, and time and will provide a light, dry wine which is pleasant, economical, and highly invigorating.

Ingredients:

- 1 quart can of natural orange juice
- 2 lbs. white sugar
- yeast
- campden tablets (ordinary "fruit-preserving" tablets — the active ingredient is sodium metabisulphate)
- 1 gallon-size glass jug
- 1 fermenting lock with cork to fit jug

The orange juice and sugar can be obtained from any supermarket; the other items from any drug store. The yeast can be of any kind but prepare it according to the instructions on the packet. Put the sugar into a large saucepan, add one pint of water, stir and bring to the boil. Allow to simmer for 25 minutes, remove from the heat, add a second pint of water, and set aside to cool. The result will be a clear, slightly golden syrup. Into the jug pour the orange juice, half the syrup, and a quart of water. The temperature of the mix should be between 80° and 90° F. Add the prepared yeast, shake well, stop the open neck with some loose wadding, and set the jug aside in a warmish place — an airing cupboard will do fine. Wait a few days. During this time the contents of the jug will be violently active with an initial ferment. If no ferment is to be seen, add more yeast. When it has quietened, add the rest of the syrup together with sufficient water to fill the container to the neck, fit the fermenting lock, and replace the jug in its warm place. The fermenting lock must be filled with water in which a campden tablet has been dissolved and the level maintained, as its purpose is to seal the wine from contact with the outside air. After eight or ten weeks the wine will begin to clear, leaving a thick sediment on the bottom of the jug. Remove the fermentation lock, add two crushed campden tablets to the wine, replace the lock, and wait for another week. The campden tablets are a sterilizing and stabilizing agent; they will kill off any still-active yeast and hasten the final clearing of the wine. When it is clear, syphon off, taking care not to disturb the sediment at the bottom of the jug. This wine, though young, is perfectly enjoyable. If you want to get a really commercial brilliance to the wine, it can be passed through a filtering medium. Before bottling add two more campden tablets* for stability.

*Campden tablets are just ordinary fruit-preserving tablets and the active ingredient is sodium metabisulphate — a salt-spoon of that will do just as well to stabilize a gallon of wine, though more won't hurt. It produces sulphur dioxide, which kills the yeast and acts as a preservative.

Putamayo (a wine of distinction)

This is a most unusual wine, with a subtle blend of tantalizing flavors and a piquancy to the tongue which defies concrete description. It is best taken with an unsweetened dry biscuit, as a clean palate is essential to its full appreciation.

Ingredients:

2 lbs. raisins	1 oz. ground cloves
2 lbs. old potatoes	1 oz. nutmeg
2 lbs. white sugar	1 tbsp. glycerine
1 lb. golden syrup	2 lemons
4 oz. wheat	1 lime
2 oz. yerba maté	Champagne yeast

Soak the wheat for two days and then coarse-grind in a mincer. Wash the potatoes, cut into small pieces, and boil gently until they are just soft. Strain and retain the water, into which put the sugar; boil until it has completely dissolved. Pressure-cook the raisins in two pints of water until they are pulped. Mix the pulped raisins, the ground wheat, the cloves, and the potato-sugar water in a large crock. Add the juice of the lemons and lime together with sufficient water to make a gallon of must. Adjust the temperature to 85° F. and add the yeast. Cover and set in a warm place for fifteen days, stirring twice a day. Strain the must through a fine nylon filter bag in order to remove as much solid matter as possible, squeezing the bag with the hands to obtain as much liquid as can be obtained. Place this in a fermenting jar, add the nutmeg and half the golden syrup. Infuse the yerba maté in sufficient water to completely fill the jar and, when cooled to 85° F., add both liquid and leaves to the container. Fit the fermenting lock and leave until all apparent activity has ceased and a thick sediment has settled on the bottom. Rack, add the glycerine, and make up the bulk with golden syrup. Wait until the wine clears, then stabilize with campden tablets and bottle in the usual way. This wine improves vastly with age, and a year, at least, should be allowed before drinking.

EDWARD WELLEN

Spaghetti Garbanzos

1 package spaghetti

1 package Spatini (or
other sauce mix, or
tin of sauce)

1 large can garbanzos
(chick peas)

1 can tomato paste

greens for salad

an Israeli *vin rouge* —
Chateau Richon

The chick peas make a good substitute for meatballs for a low-cholesterol diet.

Prepare spaghetti according to directions and while it is cooking, prepare sauce, adding chick peas. Drain spaghetti, place in large bowl. Cover with sauce and stir slightly. Serve immediately with tossed green salad and wine. Serves 4-6 amply.

KATE WILHELM

Beans For When You Want More Than Just Beans

1 lb. green beans, fresh, *or*
   2 cans Italian-type
   green beans, *or*
   2 cans whole string
   beans
6 tbsp. butter

$\frac{1}{2}$ lb. fresh mushrooms,
   caps only, sliced
$\frac{1}{4}$ lb. blanched almonds,
   whole
salt, pepper to taste

Brown almonds in butter slowly; add mushrooms and stir until they give up some of their moisture. Add beans, drained thoroughly if canned. Cover tightly if fresh beans are used and simmer until they are tender, no more than fifteen minutes. If canned beans are used, simmer about five minutes, or enough to heat through and to cook the mushrooms to the degree desired. We like them rather on the raw side. Serves 6.

The World's Biggest Crab Cake

4 eggs, separated

1 6-oz. can crab meat, or fresh crab meat to make an equivalent amount, or frozen

$\frac{1}{4}$ cup slivered onion

$\frac{1}{4}$ cup slivered water chestnuts

$\frac{1}{4}$ cup slivered celery

$\frac{1}{4}$ cup slivered scallions, tops and all

1 tbsp. soy sauce

1 slice ginger root (preserved and washed well), minced

$\frac{1}{4}$ cup stock or water, or liquid from crab plus 2 tbsp sherry

1 tbsp. oil

4 tbsp. butter

1 clove garlic (optional)

salt and pepper

Beat egg whites until peaks form; set aside. Beat yellows until thick. Add stock or liquid, salt, and pepper. Add crab. Heat oil in heavy 10-inch skillet. Add garlic, if used, and brown, then discard garlic. Add vegetables and heat through very quickly on high heat, no more than one minute. Remove from heat and stir in soy sauce to cool them slightly. Add vegetables to egg mixture. Fold in stiffly beaten whites. Heat butter until it starts to brown. Pour in egg mixture, using the same 10-inch skillet, which should be ovenproof. Cook without stirring for about 20 minutes on top of stove over medium heat, until bottom is well browned and mixture starts to look done slightly. Place in oven preheated to 400° F. and finish cooking until top is nicely browned — 10 minutes. Turn out upside down on large platter and serve either as it is or with a sauce, such as oyster sauce or mushroom sauce. (I use an ancient black cast-iron skillet for this. Makes the bottom get a nice crust without burning.)

Serves 4-6.

JACK WODHAMS

Two Inedible Limericks

To his heart through his stomach, yes, seek,
Lovelorn lass, but pray heed as I speak.
    Fed unwisely too well,
    And romancin's to hell,
He'll just burp, and then sleep for a week.

His French wizard gave Claude in his wish
For an out-of-this-world Swedish dish,
    Not puissant blonde cutie
    Rendered in tutti-frutti,
But a brass-band composed of dried fish.

Cherry and Kangaroo Nut Quizcake

4 oz. flour

1 egg, beaten in

2 tsp. gelatin

dash salt

milk

1 lb. fresh cherries, pitted

$\frac{1}{4}$ lb. kangaroo nuts*

[*Editor takes no responsibility for supplying kangaroo nuts. However, hazelnuts might make good substitute. — ED.]

If you want something different, here is one from the country districts of Australia, though it is also very much fancied by city-bound health fanatics. This dish is named "Quizcake" because of the similarity between a kangaroo nut and a cherry, so that a guessing game can be easily instituted, making this a popular and amusing dish for party occasions. Some "natural food" faddists are quite partial to this diet, and declare that it helps keep them fit and their muscles remarkably well-toned. This benefit, though, surely stems mainly from the gathering, the chase, and the subsequent wrestling. Some kangaroos get awful mad.

In a bowl, make a batter of the flour, beaten in egg, gelatin, and dash of salt. This mixture should be thinned, if it needs thinning, with milk to a creamy consistency. Thoroughly mix kangaroo nuts and pitted fresh cherries and place in a lightly waxed (greased) baking dish. Pour batter evenly over fruit-and-nut mixture and then place pan into medium oven (350° F.) and bake until crust is golden brown. May be served hot or cold.

And then there is that venerable recipe for Breast of Pterodactyl Sauté, taken from Mrs. Beatup's Cookery Wall in a cave in the Pyrenees — "First catch your pterodactyl. Then, as for lobster, dunk the creature live into a large scalding cauldron or, should you live in a serviced district, into a thermal lake, or the nearby rent-your-own boiling mud pool. Leave to simmer for three days, and then . . ." Here, unfortunately, either erosion has taken place or her chisel got blunt, and a great patch is unreadable. But on a lower part of wall she goes on (in that manner which makes her graffiti so charming) to remark the great shortage of cooks which seems to occur with strange regularity every pterodactyl season. . . .

CHELSEA QUINN YARBRO

Chicken in Port Wine Sauce

3-4 chicken breasts, halved (i.e., 6-8 halves)

1 cube ($\frac{1}{4}$ lb.) butter

3 tbsp. concentrated orange juice

$\frac{3}{4}$ cup mushrooms, sliced

3 medium leeks, the white bulb part only, thinly sliced

3 tbsp. arrowroot

dashes of mace, pepper, M.S.G., allspice, cardamon, and an infinitesimal amount of strong curry powder

1 heaping tsp. sugar

6 crushed juniper berries

5th of ruby port

3 thin-sliced lemons

First take the skin off the chicken breasts and then take the chicken meat off the bone. Throw away the skins or give them to the cat. Keep the meat in a mound somewhere while you slice up the mushrooms and leeks. Set them aside. Take a large, deep frying pan or Dutch oven, put in butter, and warm slowly until it is melted. Add the orange juice, mushrooms, leeks, and one cup of the port. Let bubble together over very low heat until they are well acquainted (roughly 5-10 minutes). Take care that the butter does not get too brown. Add the juniper berries. Now pour out another cup of the port and to it add the arrowroot, spices, and sugar. Stir well. Add *slowly* to the simmered butter, stirring frantically. Add the port slowly and continue to stir. If there is any of the arrowroot left in the cup, slosh the last of the port through it and add it to the sauce. When the whole thing is a delicious medium thin consistency, find the chicken and put it into the sauce. Cover and simmer for about 45 minutes to an hour. Fifteen minutes before removing from flame, add the lemon slices. Serve with asparagus in lemon butter and perhaps summer squash cooked with white wine and cheese. Serves about 5.

Favorite Picnic for the Beach

(Note: This must be served with good china, silver or plateware, on an acceptable tablecloth with real wine glasses or the spirit is lost.)

1 fresh cracked (and cleaned) crab per 3 people

cold pickled beets with rosemary and little onions added

stuffed eggs

celery with Cheddar cheese-sour cream filling

cherry tomatoes in red wine vinegar

1 large loaf of extra sour French bread, sliced and buttered

Italian dry salami (for people who don't like crab)

chilled champagne

For stuffed eggs: Hard-boil, peel, and halve the eggs. Remove yolks. Crush yolks, and combine with Worcestershire sauce, French mustard, turmeric, cayenne pepper, paprika, mayonnaise, ginger and dill weed. Blend together and fill whites with it.

Trudge off to your favorite beach, ocean variety preferred

where available. Spread the goodies with all due ceremony and enjoy.

The Out-of-Door Wonder

3-4 lbs. chuck roast cut off the bone into chunks

2 cups sweet vermouth

$\frac{1}{2}$ cup raisins

$\frac{1}{2}$ cup vinegar

3 tsp. sugar

2 tbsp. A-1 or similar meat sauce

$\frac{1}{4}$ tsp. powdered garlic

$\frac{1}{4}$ cup finely chopped onions

Combine ingredients two days before you intend to serve it. Let them sit together in a cool place, say, the refrigerator. Then, on the cooking day, take it out and add:

2-3 sliced red potatoes

4 medium-sized carrots, cut into fork-size

oregano, marjoram, sweet basil, bay leaves, pepper, *very* light salting, a couple of cloves, and a dash of allspice

Put all this in a large pot, cover securely, and cook over a slow fire for about 2 hours. If you are using the oven, cook in a covered heavy duty baking dish at 300° F. for $2\frac{1}{2}$ to 3 hours.

If dining indoors is more to your taste, leave out the potatoes and carrots and serve over your choice of pasta or rice. Serves 6 outdoors and 8 indoors, depending on appetites.

Panukakua

Batter:

1 dozen eggs, whipped to
a yellow froth

$\frac{3}{4}$ cup powdered sugar,
dissolved in . . .

  $1\frac{1}{2}$ cups milk

  $\frac{1}{2}$ cup flour, sifted into the
  whole mixture and
  stirred at the very last

$\frac{1}{8}$ lb. ($\frac{1}{2}$ cube) butter in a
deep baking dish or
heavy iron skillet(s)

small amount vanilla or
almond extract, if
desired

Preheat oven to 400° F.; put the baking dish(es) into it with
the butter. While this is going on, mix up the batter as described
above. Add a little vanilla or almond flavoring if you are so
inclined.

Bring the hot pans from the oven, pour in the batter quickly,
put the pans back in the oven and close the door. Let them bake
at 400° F. for 15 minutes, then turn down to 300° F. Cook for
another 30 minutes or until the top gets golden around the edges
and the center is firm, whichever comes first.

(Note: This is an old family treasure and hence fraught with
tradition, which means that the measurements are pretty irregu-
lar, i.e., how much is a double grandmother's handful? If at first
you don't succeed, play around with it for a while. It's very good
once you get the hang of it.)

Stuffed Cabbage

1 large cabbage

$1\frac{1}{4}$ lbs. ground chuck or round

$\frac{3}{4}$ lb. bulk pork or beef sausage

1 cup milk

1 cup whole ripe olives, drained

$\frac{1}{2}$ cup water chestnuts, chopped

$\frac{1}{2}$ cup tiny mushrooms, chopped

1 cup sour cream

3 cups undrained, stewed tomatoes

Fill a large pot with 5-6 cups water. Add milk and bring to a boil. Put cabbage into the pot and boil for 5 minutes. Remove, drain, and set aside. Take the ground meat, sausage, olives, water chestnuts, mushrooms, and mix thoroughly together. Your hands are best for this. When done, take the cabbage and cut the heart out at the stem. Put the meat mixture into the cabbage. You may have to secure it with a string to keep the shape. This is fine. When the cabbage is stuffed, empty out the milky water if you haven't done so already, and put the cabbage into the pot. Cover with the stewed tomatoes. Clap a lid on the whole thing and put it in the oven at 325° F. for about an hour and 45 minutes. If prepared over an open fire, be sure that the meat is completely cooked. When it is done, serve in a deep dish with the sour cream on top. This being a one-dish meal, remember that everyone will eat a lot of it unless you fill them up with French bread or pasta. If you are serving wine, you will need a full-bodied red. I prefer cabernet, but a not-too-young chianti or burgundy are fine, too.

Wassail

(This misleading Christmastime tripple is not only very good but very dangerous.)

5 quarts apricot nectar

cinnamon sticks, cloves,
    allspice berries,
    ground nutmeg,
    mace, all in a
    cheesecloth bag

1 cup sugar

14-16 eggs, whipped

5th of apricot brandy

5th apricot liqueur

5th rum

5th brandy

In a deep pot *slowly* warm the apricot nectar with the bag of spices to just the edge of simmering, stirring occasionally. Do not allow to boil.

About 15 minutes before you intend to serve this concoction, pour the hot apricot nectar into a preheated punch bowl, removing the spice bag in the process. Beat the eggs and sugar together. Cry for help. When help arrives, one of you stir the apricot juice constantly while the other of you dribbles the egg into the hot juice. Remember, a little egg at a time and much stirring. You do not want an omelette in wassail. When that is done, add the apricot brandy and liqueur. Stir the lot mightily to mix all the way down. Just before serving, add the rum and brandy. Serve hot. This should last about 30 drinkers about 5 hours.

If apricots are not your thing, it can be done with peaches and peach-flavored brandy and liqueur.

Warning: because this is hot, people will tend not to feel the drink. Best serve in small portions.

INDEX

D

E

vegetables (*see also by name*)
   in salad, 153
   nituke, 105
venison, 19-20
   sevagram, 21
vitamin deficiency, 146

W

wassail, 195
Welsh rabbit, 47
wine
   chicken in port, 190

fish steamed in, 38
lamb and onion in, 112
orange, 181
putamayo, 183
turkey drumsticks in, 38

Y

yeast deficiency, 146
Yorkshire pudding, 52

Z

zucchini, 128